Praise for
A Modest But Crucial Hero

"In *A Modest But Crucial Hero*, Rev. Judson Stone shares the inspiring story of his great-great-uncle, Rev. George Stone, who in 1898 left his comfortable home in New York to travel to Arabia to share God's love with his Muslim brothers and sisters. While the book takes into consideration the lack of political correctness of the time in relation to missionary efforts, it also shows a young man whose devotion to God and his love for others cannot be questioned, especially since he made the ultimate sacrifice. Thank you, Rev. Stone, for sharing Rev. Stone's story."

— Tyler R. Tichelaar, PhD and Award-Winning Author of
Kawbawgam: The Chief, The Legend, The Man

"I thoroughly enjoyed *A Modest But Crucial Hero*. This is a masterful account of Rev. George E. Stone's inspiring dedication to Jesus Christ which ultimately took him to the mission field of the Arabian Peninsula where he laid down his life in His service.... George is the kind of role model of which the Church is always in need—someone who practices self-denial, takes up the cross, and follows Jesus wherever He may lead."

— Rev. Adam Simnowitz, Minister and Missionary, Assemblies of God

"With the bravado of youth and a Christian conviction of considerable maturity, George Stone set sail in the fall of 1898 for the Persian Gulf country of Bahrain. There he readied himself for a lifetime of evangelical service. In early 1899, he was reassigned to the mission outpost of Muscat, Oman, where he served for a matter of months. By early summer, his health was compromised, and in late June, he passed away.

Three generations later, his great-great-nephew learned of this martyred ancestor and wanted to know more."

— Donald A. Luidens, PhD, Van Raalte Institute, Director; Professor Emeritus of Sociology, Hope College, Holland, Michigan

"Every now and again, in the pages of a well-written book, we are introduced to someone whom history ought to know better. In telling the life story of G. E. Stone, his great-great-nephew Judson Stone has placed all students of missionary history, and pioneering philanthropy, in his debt. With a deep love for the Arab people of his day, G. E. Stone lived a life of compassion, sacrifice, and ultimately, martyrdom—a life of service to others, in a place far from America's shores. In the twenty-five years of his life, he won the admiration of many leaders in the modern missionary movement and won the hearts of all who knew him. Judson Stone's biography tells us why...."

— Kevin Belmonte, Biographer, Lead Script and Historical Consultant for the Film *Amazing Grace*

"*A Modest But Crucial Hero* is a call to remember. In Psalm 78, the children of Israel…forget their roots and their own story. Forgetfulness leads to disconnectedness and unbelief. Remembering leads to gratitude and renewed faith. *A Modest But Crucial Hero* is a compelling read and an inspiring story, full of well-researched details that draw the reader back to a different time in history…one well worth remembering."

— Sean Lambert, YWAM San Diego/Baja

"For years I've wondered what had happened to George Stone. While serving as the director of Al Amana Centre in Muscat, I would bring study-abroad students on tours of Oman. The Cove Cemetery was one of our stops nearly every semester where we would visit the graves of missionaries. I knew a bit about the stories of Bishop Valpy French, Peter Zwemer, and Sharon Thoms, but I knew very little about George Stone, only that he had died tragically at the age of twenty-five. What a gift this book is to a long incomplete chapter in the history of the Arabian Mission. I was captivated as I read and intrigued to see details of George's experience that were common to my own. His story brought me in touch with the tragedy of his death and the impact of his life."

— Rev. Douglas Leonard, Lead Pastor, Hopewell Reformed Church, Hopewell Junction, New York

"Any who have studied the Christian mission movement over the last two centuries are familiar with the Student Volunteer Movement (SVM), a movement in the late nineteenth and early twentieth centuries that launched more than 20,000 young people into cross-cultural missions… but few of us know the story of any of the actual SVM volunteers. This book is one of those stories. Judson Stone opens our eyes to the real-life sacrifices that George made…that would eventually take his life at age twenty-five. This is an inspirational book about one man's exemplary life—fully devoted to Jesus, dedicated to loving those who were far from God, and willing to live a life of sacrifice."

— Paul Borthwick, Senior Consultant, Development Associates International; Author of *Western Christians in Global Mission: What's the Role of the North American Church*

"Jud Stone has tackled this biography in his typically thorough and insightful way, as a work of love and respect for his great-great-uncle. This is a book you'll want to read."

— Daryl E. Witmer, AIIA Institute, Monson, Maine

"What I appreciated in *A Modest But Crucial Hero* was the reminder of the fallen heroes and heroines of the faith, who have in many cases gone unnamed and unrecognized. Rev Judson Stone has brought to life one of those modest and crucial heroes, Rev. George Stone, and has given a lasting legacy to his life's work. Like his savior, Rev. George Stone's life was cut short, and the true impact of his committed and consecrated life will not be known in this world. Rev. George Stone's life was inspirational to those who met and especially those who knew him."

— Pastor Charles C Wilson, PhD, The Chapel at Crosspoint, Santa Rosa Beach, Florida

A MODEST BUT CRUCIAL HERO

The Life and Legacy of
Rev. George E. Stone
(1873-1899)

REV. JUDSON I. STONE
D. MINISTRY

A Modest But Crucial Hero
The Life and Legacy of Rev. George E. Stone (1873-1899)

Copyright © 2023 by Rev. Judson I. Stone, D. Ministry. All rights reserved.

Published by:

Aviva Publishing
Lake Placid, NY
(518) 523-1320
www.AvivaPubs.com

All Rights Reserved. No part of this book may be used or reproduced in any manner whatsoever without the expressed written permission of the author.

Address all inquiries to:

Rev. Judson I. Stone. D. of Ministry
Jis1908@sbcglobal.net
https://JudsonIStone.com

ISBN: 978-1-63618-278-0
Library of Congress Control Number: 2023911833

Editor: Tyler Tichelaar, Superior Book Productions
Cover Design and Interior Book Layout: Fusion Creative Works

Every attempt has been made to properly source all quotes.

Printed in the United States of America

First Edition

2 4 6 8 10 12

Dedicated with gratitude to
Howard Kliever,
who as a young Air Force airman in August 1970,
explained the good news of Jesus Christ to me
and prayed with me to receive Him into my heart
a few weeks before I entered college.
Howard's help, and Christ's answer to my prayer,
changed my life to the glory of God.

Acknowledgments

I thank God for the privilege of researching and writing about my great-great-uncle, the Rev. George E. Stone. I learned so much more about him, his family, their hometown, the Arabian Mission, the Persian Gulf region, the world, and Islam.

My wife gave me freedom to invest time in the project. She listened to all my discoveries, ideas, questions, and frustrations.

My brother David financed the trip to Oman. His assistance and encouragement were priceless.

My brother Stephen's prayers and encouragement made the visit to Oman that much more enjoyable for me and David.

Many other people and organizations contributed to my research: Carol Norville Berning (carolberning.com);

Natalie Dardaris, Onondaga Hill, New York Town Historian and member of the Onondaga Hill Presbyterian Church that George served while in seminary;

Grant McKenzie, student at Hope College and a research assistant;

Archive.org;

NYHistoricNewspapers.org;

Walton County Library (FL);

Adam Simnowitz, ordained minister and writer for *The Journal of Biblical Missiology;*

Mark E. Tillson, Jr., Special Collections Coordinator, Burke Library, Hamilton College;

Margaret Thickstun, the Jane Watson Irwin Professor of Literature, Hamilton College;

Gale Stone, my cousin and a Latin expert;

John Treadwell, cousin, family historian, and archivist;

Mexico, New York Historical Society and Judy Greenway, Town Historian;

Rev. Douglas Leonard, pastor of Hopewell Junction Reformed Church, New York and former Director of the Al Amana Centre for Muslim and Christian Relations, Oman;

Andrew Choi, First Rate, Inc., for arranging flights to Oman;

Elizabeth Pallitto, PhD, Archivist, Reformed Church in America Archives;

Tyler R. Tichelaar, PhD, editor and manuscript advisor;

The members of the Destin Word Weavers International Writers Chapter who critiqued large portions of the manuscript, helping me turn facts into a story;

The many authors who went before me in researching and writing for my benefit;

Finally, my many prayer partners around the world.

Contents

Preface	15
Introduction	19
PART I - A MAN OF OUR HOPES	21
Chapter 1: Growing Up in Mexico, New York	23
Chapter 2: Hamilton College	37
Chapter 3: Ministerial Training at Auburn Seminary	47
Chapter 4: Prepared for the Work of Service	49
Chapter 5: Clarity about God's Calling	55
Chapter 6: Preparing for the Mission Field	61
Chapter 7: Farewell to Mexico, New York	67
PART II - JOURNEY TO ARABIA	71
Chapter 8: A *Majestic* Trip to Great Britain	73
Chapter 9: La Belle France	87
Chapter 10: Introduction to the Orient	91
Chapter 11: Hello, India	99
PART III - BAHRAIN	105
Chapter 12: On the Mission Field	107
Chapter 13: Arabic, Arabic, Arabic	113
Chapter 14: The Awkward Squad	125
Chapter 15: Take Up the Work	143
PART IV - MUSCAT, OMAN	151
Chapter 16: An International Showdown	153
Chapter 17: House Repairs and Slave School	159
Chapter 18: Eyes on Calendar and Thermometer	173

PART V - DEATH AND BURIAL	179
Chapter 19: A Most Grievous Blow	181
Chapter 20: Memorial Service and Tributes	189
Chapter 21: More Tributes	195
Chapter 22: The Family Carries On	203
PART VI - REV. GEORGE E. STONE'S LEGACY	209
Chapter 23: His Legacy in Literature	211
Chapter 24: Willing for It to Be So	227
Bibliography	235
Endnotes	241
About the Author	277
More Books by Rev. Judson I. Stone	279

Important People in the Story

George Washington Stone: George's father; a merchant

Sophia Ransom Slack Stone: George's mother

Frederick, Lydia, Ernest, Harry Stone: George's siblings; Lydia died shortly before George's birth

Benjamin Stone: Uncle to George; a merchant

Samuel Stone: Uncle to George, a merchant

Rev. George Bayless: Pastor of First Presbyterian Church, Mexico, New York

Mr. Henry Humphries: Mexico *Independent* proprietor, editor; Sunday School Superintendent

Arthur Berry: George's childhood friend; Methodist missionary in Japan

Rev. Anthony N. Petersen: George's college and seminary classmate

Rev. Dr. M. Woolsey Stryker: President, Hamilton College

Rev. Samuel M. Zwemer: Cofounder, Arabian Mission; George's mentor

Mrs. Amy Zwemer: Wife of Samuel

Rev. James Cantine: Cofounder, Arabian Mission

Rev. Peter J. Zwemer: Arabian Mission personnel; brother to Samuel; founded Rescued Slave Boys School, Muscat, Oman

Rev. Dr. Henry N. Cobb: Reformed Church in America, Foreign Missions Corresponding Secretary

Rev. Frederick Barny and Mrs. Margaret Rice Barny: Arabian Mission personnel

Elias: Arabian Mission staff

Yusef Seesoo: Arabian Mission staff; George's Arabic teacher

Sultan Faysal bin-Turki: Ruler of Oman in Muscat

Major C. G. F. Fagan: British Consul in Muscat, Oman

Archibald MacKirdy: American Vice Consul; mail, import, export agent

David A. Stone: Brother to the author; cofounder, First Rate, Inc., Arlington, Texas

Stephen M. Stone: Brother to the author; ordained minister, retired project manager

Preface

The origin of this biography of the Reverend George E. Stone arose by reading the brief tribute to him in *The History of the Arabian Mission*. The book sat on my parents' bookshelf in the early 1970s.[1] My relatively new faith in Jesus Christ had given me an interest in missions. My heart became enthralled with this great-great-uncle's brief story. The tribute was not extensive, but it planted the seed for this biography.

George Erwin Stone (September 1, 1873—June 26, 1899) was a twenty-five-year-old missionary with the Arabian Mission in Manama, Bahrain and Muscat, Oman. He joined thousands of young men and women who entered the Student Volunteer Movement by pledging to serve in other countries to spread the good news of Jesus Christ and to establish or strengthen Christ's Church in them. He was appointed a missionary in early 1898 before graduating from Auburn Theological Seminary in Auburn, New York. He died in Birka, north of Muscat, and was buried in the English Cove Cemetery in Muscat.

George's oldest brother, Frederick Stone (1867 – 1921), was my great-grandfather. Their other two brothers, Ernest and Harry, died in 1968 and 1970, respectively. I met them in the 1960s when my knowledge of and interest in George was non-existent. I did not think to ask these aged great-great-uncles about their brother George.

Several years later in 1984, a great-nephew of George, Douglas Courtright, learned of my interest in our common ancestor. He gave me his family's scrapbook that contained the printed excerpts of George's letters to his parents. I wrote to the Bahrain Consulate in Washington, DC, in October 1984 to inquire about visiting the island country where George began his missionary service in Arabic language training. I did not follow up on the matter.

As a student at Gordon-Conwell Theological Seminary in 1975-78, I studied under missions professor Dr. J. Christy Wilson, Jr. I learned later that he had personal and professional interests in Dr. Samuel Zwemer, a cofounder of the Arabian Mission. Dr. Wilson's father wrote a biography of Samuel Zwemer in 1952.[2] Dr. Wilson, Jr. served as a missionary in Afghanistan for more than two decades until 1973. Around 1990, I shared the family scrapbook with Dr. Wilson and talked to him about George and Zwemer.

I renewed my research about George in 2014-16 when I wrote a biography of my father.[3] I included information about George as part of our family's heritage. Before I retired in March 2018, I wrote a note to myself that I wanted to visit his grave. I discovered a picture of his grave online and began to plan the trip for early 2020. I also connected with a Tennessee artist, Carol Berning, whose husband is a descendant of George's aunt (and a distant cousin to me). Carol sent me photos of their family scrapbook, which includes George's travel letters. The scrapbook is almost identical to the one I received from Douglas Courtright and dates from the same period. I learned at this time that George's letters were accessible on the New York Historical Newspaper website. I immediately began to study them.

The Mexico, New York *Independent* newspaper became my primary source about George. The owner and editor of the paper, Mr. Henry Humphries, was a close friend of the Stone family and attended the Presbyterian Church with them. He served as the Superintendent of the Sunday School during George's youth. He mentored him in the Christian faith directly and indirectly. Humphries served as one of the best advocates for George's missionary calling and short period of service by printing excerpts of his letters. If there had not been a Mr. Humphries, we would know little about George and his family.

My two brothers and I visited George's grave in Muscat on Saturday, January 25, 2020. Gratitude to God filled my heart when my dream to visit the grave became a reality. Besides visiting George's grave, we attended the Anglican worship service at the Protestant Church in Muscat, visited a married couple doing business and learned that George's legacy lives on to this day.

I talked to my brothers about writing a biography and asked them to pray for the project. Research began in earnest after we returned home. The coronavirus pandemic closed many facilities that contained pertinent material about George's affiliation with the Arabian Mission. The research I did do revealed that he is mentioned in many studies about the Arabian Mission, studies that have been conducted into the 2000s.

My objective in writing a biography of George is to honor this modest but crucial hero. His story gathers together information about this brave young man who chose to serve near the birthplace of Islam in the attempt to reach Arabia with the good news of Jesus Christ. George was convinced that Islam's portrayal and admiration of Jesus of Nazareth as a prophet and the Messiah failed to embrace his full identity as the Son of God and the Savior of the world through his death and resurrection.

The book is divided into six parts. Part One introduces the reader to George and his family, education, and volunteering. Part Two traces his journey to the mission field through his letters sent home during the trip. Part Three covers George's brief Arabic language studies in Bahrain. Part Four describes his service and death in Oman. Part Five reports on the Stone family's response to George's death. Part Six examines his legacy in literature from 1900 to the present.

September 1 is the 150th anniversary of George's birth. The modern world is different from the one he grew up in. Some readers will love and respect him for his courage, theological convictions, and assessments of Islam. Others will loathe him for his Western civilization arrogance, evangelical faith, and opinions of Islam. I have tried to let him speak for himself through his own words from his letters. I used extensive portions of his letters printed in the Mexico *Independent*. The page numbers in the footnotes for the newspaper are listed as the page numbers on the New York Historic Newspapers website. I kept the quotations as true to form as possible, except where I thought changes improved or clarified the quotations. Every mention of Mexico always refers to Mexico, New York.

Introduction

"Stone dead!" declared the two-word telegram from Muscat, Oman to the United States on June 29, 1899. Such a blunt message about the Rev. George E. Stone shocked the Arabian Mission office personnel. The message filled their minds with many questions of how, when, and where. Several weeks passed before they obtained additional information about his death on June 26. The message was forwarded to George's hometown pastor in Mexico, New York. He informed George's parents. Condolences to the Stone family poured into Mexico, expressing disbelief, sadness, and tributes about their son.

George's coworker, mentor, and a cofounder of the Arabian Mission, the Rev. Samuel M. Zwemer, stated in his memorial tribute to George that he was "the man of our hopes during the months we lived together in the same cramped quarters at Bahrain."[1] He wrote this tribute for three reasons. First, George's presence on the field took on a greater significance for the Mission shortly after he and the Zwemers arrived in Bahrain in October 1898. They received news that Rev. Zwemer's younger brother and coworker in the Arabian Mission, Rev. Peter Zwemer, had died October 18 in the United States from an illness contracted in Oman. George's arrival provided fresh assurance that the Mission was supposed to press on in its objective of reaching the heartland of Islam with the good news of Jesus Christ. A second reason Samuel viewed George as a man of their hopes included his disciplined earnestness in learning Arabic, his adaptability to harsh living conditions, his sociability on the long journey to Bahrain, and his sense of humor. The third factor in him being the man of hope for the Mission pertained to his intellectual strength, numerous skills and talents, and commitment to help the Arabian Mission fulfill its objective. Where did this young man of hope come from? Let's find out.

PART I

A MAN OF OUR HOPES

CHAPTER 1

Growing Up in Mexico, New York

The United States contains ten towns named Mexico in South Carolina, Pennsylvania, Ohio, Maine, Maryland, Kentucky, Indiana, Florida, Missouri, and New York. George's story began in Mexico, New York. Mexico is located at the eastern end of Lake Ontario, three miles inland. The town was organized in 1792 and went through several changes over the years. It originally consisted of parts of the present day Oswego, Onondaga, and Cortland Counties. It is called the Mother of Towns because its original immense land area was partitioned over many years into twenty other towns. The town's name changed as did its territory. The names included Mexico, Village of Vera Cruz, Mexicoville, and the Village of Mexico, which was incorporated in 1851.[1] The town proper is sixteen miles east of Oswego and forty-five miles northwest of Syracuse. It is composed of the Town of Mexico and the Village of Mexico.

George's ancestors sailed to the New World from England in 1635 and settled in Watertown, Massachusetts. Nearly two hundred years later, his grandparents, Isaac and Lydia Stone, arrived in Mexico with six children from Bridport, Vermont in November 1826. They were on their way west to the Western Reserve in northern Ohio. They stopped in Mexico to visit Lydia's sister. Lydia was pregnant with number seven, and with winter approaching, they decided to stay until the next spring.

The winter postponement of their journey west gave the Stones time to become acquainted with Mexico. When spring arrived, along with their newest child, they decided to stay. Isaac was a tanner. Over the course of ten years, they lived in several houses because their family grew to twelve children. Their eleventh child, George Washington, was born in 1836. He became the father of George Erwin, the subject of this book. George, the father, became a merchant like his older brothers.

Mexico's population fluctuated between 1,205 and 1,359 during young George's era.[2] Main Street was a dirt road. Rain made the town's dirt roads treacherous. Large snowfalls hampered travel by horses and wagons. The Mexico Hotel provided accommodations for visitors. The town had a planing mill, door-sash-blind factory, sawmill, grist mill, and casket company. A Town Hall was built in 1878 that provided a large auditorium for theatrical and musical shows. Mexico Academy used it for programs.

Mexico's connections to the outside world increased with the addition of the telegraph before the Civil War and rail service in 1865. The telephone made its appearance in 1881, but few homes used one in the 1890s. Kerosene lamps provided streetlight at night. In 1887, a few electric lights were installed in several businesses. Roller skating in the Town Hall entertained young and old. Natural gas and oil wells were drilled, but they did not prove profitable.[3] The region consisted of many prosperous farms and apple orchards.

Mexico's geographical location meant the "lake effect" influenced the weather patterns and conditions. The northeasterly moving weather included wind, rain, snow, humidity, and unpredictable sudden changes. Humidity made summer days and nights muggy. Temperatures ranged from highs in the 80s to low 90s Fahrenheit during the summer to sub-zero temperatures in the winter. The chilly to cold season ran from October to April. The Stone boys learned early to shovel snow to make paths to the barn and street.

George W. and Sophia Ransom Slack married in 1866 about a year after her first husband died. Rev. Isaac Slack and Sophia had lived in Newton, Iowa, where he had been a Presbyterian minister. He died less than a year after their wedding. Rev. Slack's family and the Stone family were friends. George W. and Sophia's first son Frederick was in born 1867; daughter Lydia in 1869; and son Ernest in 1870. Their youngest son, Harry, was born in 1875. Four-year-old Lydia died several weeks before George was born in 1873.

The townsfolk established the Mexico Academy in 1826. It was the first secondary school in Oswego County admitted to the State of New York education system.[4] The town had several elementary schools that fed the Academy. Georgie,[5] as his relatives and friends called him, walked with his three brothers on the dirt roads from the family house on Spring Street to the brick #8 schoolhouse on the corners of Church and Madison Streets. As teens, they moved to the Academy on Main Street, one block north and three blocks west from their house. Black Creek was the rear boundary of the school grounds. The big red brick building with its two white columns loomed before George each day as he walked to the front door. The columns never grew taller as his own height increased with age.

George had blue eyes, dark brown hair neatly parted on the left, long bushy eyebrows, and thick lips. His ears protruded out like his oldest brother Frederick's ears. Mr. Stone expected his sons to be obedient and was a strong disciplinarian. The four brothers disobeyed periodically and received their father's corporal punishment when necessary.[6]

George and his brothers played together on Spring Street and with school friends. They went sliding in Mr. Simpson's orchard in the winter.[7] Baseball was becoming popular at this time. Ice skating advanced with the invention of all-steel skate blades in 1850, and these activities gave the boys great pleasure. The earliest version of American football also took hold as an up-and-coming sport during George's lifetime.

The Stone boys lived next door to their uncle Benjamin. They had a barn and a woodshed. The yard had a large, sweet apple tree, greasy pippin apple tree, and Bartlett pear tree. Later, the boys added a wild cherry tree to the small orchard. The family raised Plymouth Rock chickens.[8] George and his brothers cared for the chickens and gathered the eggs. The boys helped plant, cultivate, and weed the garden with their mother. George watched his mother can vegetables in the kitchen. Of course, the family horses needed tending too. George learned to feed, groom, and hitch them to the carriage to transport them to Sunday worship and other outings. The boys devoured Uncle Dean Davis' chickens at Thanksgiving dinners following their outdoor play.[9]

Music influenced George's home life and the various religious and community settings. He learned to play several instruments, including the piano, melodeon, and cello. Time devoted to lessons and practicing developed his proficiency, and he used his skills regularly.

Wood stoves heated the house. A coal stove was added in the sitting room around 1886 or '87 when a coal furnace was installed in the basement.[10] Mr. Stone bought several cords of word and piled them between the two apple trees to let them dry out before the boys wheeled them into the woodshed, piling them to the roof. They stocked the house with firewood in boxes next to each stove. On cold days, the boys jumped out of bed in the morning and grabbed their clothes to dress around the warm kitchen stove. The fire was allowed to die out each night to save fuel. After the furnace installation, more of the house was used by the family and visitors during the cold season.

The house consisted of a parlor, sitting room, dining room, bedrooms, and kitchen. As a young boy, George slept in a bed with his older brother Ernest. The kitchen was at the rear, or north side, of the house. Under its floor was a large cistern that fed a water pump located at the long kitchen sink. A well and pump to draw water were also located on the outside porch that they enclosed each fall to protect the pump from the cold.

Come spring, Mrs. Stone used the wood ashes to make a soft lye soap for laundry and scrubbing. It was too harsh for general use. Carpets needed seasonal cleaning too. Mrs. Stone used the boys' strength to remove the carpets and hang them on the clotheslines for a good beating and airing.[11]

Hanging lamps provided lighting for the house. They were raised and lowered by chains to light and to extinguish the flames. The lamp over the dining table was stationary. Silver hand lamps were also used indoors. The lamps were another source of heat on a cold day or night. The hanging lamps gave the boys room on the table to do their homework. Mrs. Stone sat in the room with her work basket while the boys did their work. She knitted all their stockings, mittens, and other items. She used other women to assist with the housework. George's college roommate, Anthony Petersen, spent a few days at the Stones' house in the early 1890s and described it as a home with love, purity, faith, and piety.[12]

George saw and chatted with various kinds of peddlers who traveled from town to town by foot, horse, or wagon, attempting to sell such things as needles, buttons, lace, tonics, rags, jewelry, extracts, and medicines.[13]

Mr. and Mrs. Stone were Republicans and abstained from alcohol. Eight presidents served during George's lifetime, six of whom were Republicans. Grover Cleveland was the lone Democratic President, serving two terms with Republican Benjamin Harrison separating Cleveland's two terms. Mr. Stone donated cloth from his store for Mrs. Stone to make a Benjamin Harrison banner during the 1888 presidential campaign. The lettering on the banner was done by the painters who were painting Benjamin Stone's house next door. Each morning, the family proudly raised the banner.[14]

The Stones were active members of the First Presbyterian Church. George's grandparents, Isaac and Lydia, were founding members when the Mexico Presbyterian Church was organized in 1830. Isaac served as the Sunday School Superintendent and established Sunday Schools in various districts of the town. Several Stones are memorialized in the sanctuary's stained-glass windows. The windows reminded young George of his religious heritage after they were installed when he was seven years old. Mr. Stone served on the Board of Trustees and represented the church at various Presbytery meetings. Mrs. Stone belonged to the Women's Missionary Society. Forty-five years after George's death, the church's chapel was renovated and dedicated in memory of Isaac.[15]

George grew spiritually at home and under the leadership of three pastors: Rev. James P. Stratton (1870-1877), who baptized George as an infant; Rev. John A. Lewis (1879-1881); and Rev. George Bayless (1881-1903).[16] Rev. Bayless welcomed him into church membership. Mr. Henry Humphries, owner and editor of the Mexico *Independent*, served as the church's Sunday School Superintendent from 1867 to 1910. George was one of his lambs.

Rev. Bayless recalled that when about eleven years of age, between September 1884 to September 1885, George began to realize that God had a claim upon his life. Later, he accepted the duty to be about his Master's work and consecrated himself to his Lord's service. He was inclined to a ministerial vocation as a teenager, and his understanding of this call matured as did his physical, intellectual, and spiritual development. Rev. Bayless never forgot the beauty and steadfastness of George's consecration.[17]

Rev. George Bayless
1881-1903

From Sesquicentennial Celebration booklet,
First Presbyterian Church, 1960.

George attended the church membership training in early 1885. The class reviewed the Bible, Jesus Christ, God, salvation, eternal life, and what church membership meant. George appeared before the Session of the church, with thirteen other people, on Saturday, April 4. They were examined regarding their Christian experience and intention to live as sincere Christians. The next morning in the worship service, the fourteen candidates assented to the church's articles of faith and entered a covenant with the church. The church welcomed them into membership, and they partook of their first communion.

George studied the Bible under the tutelage of Sunday School teachers. Mr. Humphries, who saw him advance from an eight-year-old boy to manhood, first served in the church's infant department for six years before his election to the Superintendency. Assisted by other workers, including one of George's aunts, the department grew to 100.[18] During Humphries' years as the Superintendent, the school sprang to life because he made it interesting. He had a genius for incorporating new things and new stories.[19]

Humphries was English and had worked in Sunday Schools in England before immigrating to the United States. He was short, possessed a wiry personality, and in his later years, was slightly stooped and always wore a shawl.[20] He possessed a golden heart, and he lived a life of kindness.[21] Eleven young men from the church entered some form of ministry partly due to his leadership.[22] He influenced George's yes to Jesus Christ by his life.

Henry Humphries. Courtesy Mexico (NY) Historical Society.

The local newspaper also fed George's faith and optimism for it promoted religious faith and a positive outlook in life. At least four of George's relatives worked for the *Independent*: Walter Chester Stone, proprietor of the Camden *Advocate*; Charles L. Stone, a successful lawyer in Syracuse and Hamilton College Board member; Rev. Carlos H. Stone, headmaster at the boys school in Cornwall-on-the-Hudson, New York; and Junius B. Stone.[23]

Other churches contributed to Mexico's spiritual vitality. Baptist, Methodist, Episcopalian, and Catholic churches existed while George grew up. The Baptist, Methodist, and Presbyterian churches cooperated amicably. This cooperation influenced George's cooperative attitude in various ways.

George possessed an early spiritual vitality and sensitivity to God's work in his life. This led me to think about my spiritual journey. Like George, I attended church with my parents and brothers, joined a Presbyterian church, and received God's call to Christian ministry as a vocation. George's spiritual consecration, however, arose earlier than mine. My desire to know God lasted a brief moment as a twelve year old at Forest Home Christian Conference Center in southern California. The thought came and went. Six years later, a young airman in the Air Force, Howard Kliever, helped me trust in Jesus Christ for salvation. He used the little tract *Have You Heard of the Four Spiritual Laws?* I knew some of the things contained in the booklet because of my religious upbringing, but the day I met with Howard, all the training plus the timing of our conversation contributed to me praying with him to trust in Jesus Christ for the forgiveness of my sins, and for Christ to become the Lord of my life. Experientially, it was uneventful, but consequentially, it was life changing.

The booklet stated that God loved me and had a wonderful plan for my life. My sin separated me from God and prevented me from knowing God's plan. God's Son Jesus Christ died for my sins and was raised from the dead to bridge my separation from God and his plan for me. I needed to personally ask God to forgive me, trust in Jesus Christ's death and resurrection, and receive him into my life as Lord and Savior. Howard and I prayed together for me to become a follower of Christ. Within a few days, I noticed a brand-new awareness of God, delighted in reading and studying the Bible, and attempted to share my new relationship with Jesus with others.

As George grew physically and spiritually, he saw his father leave the house in the morning to open his merchandise store on Main Street. Mr. Stone started out in business as a partner with his older brother Samuel before owning his own store with various partners. He added a tailoring department in the 1870s. A customer's letter to the *Independent* in May 1879 declared, "I called into the store of G. W. Stone & Co., the proprietors, of which I have long known and respected, as candid, honest men...."[24]

Mr. Stone bought ads in the weekly *Independent* newspaper, and so did twenty-four-year-old son Frederick. He sold White Russian and Yellow Globe turnip plants. Interested customers left their orders at the store.[25] Son Ernest worked at the store in 1893 as the agent for the Victor bicycle.[26] He moved to Battle Creek, Michigan, and worked at a store owned by a former employee of Mr. Stone's. Ernest returned to New York and joined Frederick as a partner in a dry goods store in Dolgeville, New York.

George attended the Academy like his brothers. His oldest brother Frederick was declared valedictorian for the 1884 class to break a tie.[27] The Academy's Collegiate Preparatory Course prepared George well for the academic rigors at Hamilton College. He studied Latin, physiology, philosophy, Greek and Roman mythology, geography, *Caesar's Commentaries*, US history, rhetoric, algebra, Greek, Virgil, *Anabasis* by Xenophon, geometry, Cicero, and general history.[28] His uncle Benjamin S. Stone was the President of the Board of Trustees from 1878 to 1895 and George's father was the Treasurer for many years.[29]

George excelled academically. He scored well in New York educational tests called the Regents Examinations. George received honors in the Examinations in algebra, physical geography, American history, physics advanced, physics elementary, Cicero's *Orations*, and Xenophon's *Anabasis*. He participated in a Friday evening rhetoric program in October 1888. He studied great historical men and authored an essay titled "Great Men."

Mexico Academy Graduation Photo. Personal collection.

Two descriptions of George appear in his 1889 Class *Annual.* In the Class Prophecy, he is described as tall, rather lank, jaded, and playing the hand-organ. "Jaded," meaning fatigued by overwork, would be truly prophetic of him ten years later. Another classmate wrote five couplets that portray him as kind, polished, and pure:

> We have a *Stone*, though, not a rock,
> For surely he would no one shock.
>
> Not in the boulder's huge rough sides,
> Kind friends, the truest worth resides,
>
> But in some small and polished stone,
> Like diamonds, there is worth alone.

> And you, dear friends, I would assure,
> This one, with mind polished and pure,
>
> Is worth far more than diamonds bright,
> Which cannot shine save in the light.[30]

George chose a couplet from Henry Wadsworth Longfellow's *Tales of a Wayside Inn* for his delineation, a personal description, in the *Annual*:

> A youth was there, of quiet ways,
> A Student of old books and days,[31]

The couplet suggests he tended to be quiet and an avid reader.

George wrote the Class History for the *Annual*, which shows that he garnered respect from his classmates and the faculty. The class started out with twenty-three students but finished with twelve. George wrote with humility, "we all doubtless see many places where we could have made improvement." The challenges that *Caesar's Commentaries* gave the class were unforgettable. George's Latin skills led him to convert Caesar's singulars into plurals "venimus, vidimus, vicimus…Victory is ours at last. In oratory, in science, in classics, we are conquerors."[32] Two classmates had died and the surviving members "find comfort… that they are in mansions of rest." The graduates encountered other hardships, but they:

> press boldly forward with fresh courage. In future years, when the fame of '89 as lawyers, physicians, ministers, or even senators shall have spread abroad, we will recall the happy days spent here in preparation for future greatness.[33]

The mention of ministers included himself. His humor came through in his reference to "forced marches to the principal's room" and Caesar was a stubborn enemy who was "compelled to surrender."

George introduced "Louis Kossuth"[34] to the audience in his graduation ceremony speech. He touched on something of contemporary significance:

> The struggle of men and nations for civil and religious liberty are of the greatest interest. The motto of Kossuth—There are no difficulties to him, who wills.[35]

He reviewed the struggle between Hungary and Austria and highlighted:

> three important characteristics of Kossuth—patriotism, love of liberty, and unswerving trust in God. Kossuth taught that morality and patriotism were the pillars of government. His example was worthy of imitation.[36]

George's Uncle Benjamin stood on the platform with Principal More, who presented George his diploma and told him, "Like Louis Kossuth, be a patriot, loyal to country, to God and to self."[37]

The 1889 class motto was *Finis coronat opus*—The end crowns the work.[38] It held special significance for the class, but it also foreshadowed George's life's end that would crown his short life.

George enrolled in the post-graduate course at the Academy[39] in anticipation of college. He joined the Teachers' Class.[40] This program gave him practical instruction in the science and art of teaching.[41]

CHAPTER 2

Hamilton College

George continued his formal education in contrast to his two older brothers who became merchants like their father. He attended Hamilton College in Clinton, New York, and Auburn Theological Seminary in Auburn, New York. Hamilton is in Clinton about ten miles southwest of Utica, and Auburn west of Syracuse.[1] Several of George's relatives also attended these schools. His cousins William G. Stone (1875) and Carlos Stone (1878) graduated from the college.[2] His brother Harry and cousin Warren S. Stone graduated from both the college and seminary after him. George's mother's first husband, Rev. Comfort Israel Slack, was an 1860 Hamilton and 1863 Auburn graduate.[3] Her brother George Ransom graduated from Auburn in 1860. Warren served as an instructor at Auburn in Elocution and Music in 1911-1913.[4]

Hamilton College's origins go back to Hamilton-Oneida Academy. Its purpose was to serve the Oneida Indians and white children. After the founder's death, the school was renamed Hamilton College to honor Alexander Hamilton's support and service to the Academy as a trustee. George received a traditional classical education that included languages, philosophy, religion, history, and mathematics. It put a great emphasis on rhetoric and elocution. The rigorous curriculum required hard work.

The campus is located on College Hill. The New York, Ontario and Western train station in town was about one-and-a-half miles from the college. The walk up the hill challenged George's stamina. The arbor halfway up the hill provided him with a rest area. The hilltop gave George a beautiful panoramic view of the Mohawk Valley. The dormitories were old and inadequate. He lived in North Hall.[5] His class started with forty-eight members and gained two more, but only thirty graduated. Fraternity dances, house parties, theatricals, glee and banjo clubs, and the college quartet provided social opportunities. His class inaugurated the Sophomore Hop and graduation caps and gowns. The library housed 30,000 volumes.[6] Regular chapel services provided spiritual nurture.

Athletic activities started out as extracurricular activities, but eventually intercollegiate football began in 1890.[7] George served as the team's manager in 1894 when the team went 0-4.[8] He took great interest in the game, had remarkable business acumen, and was popular among the students.[9] He was also a Vice President of the Athletic Union that year.

George is wearing the suit and bow tie. Courtesy of Hamilton College Archives.

Anthony Petersen, a roommate, reported that George was not a graceful dancer, but he played tennis, baseball, and football intramurally. As a scholar, he might have been the valedictorian if he had not devoted himself to many other responsibilities on campus.[10]

George enhanced his spiritual development by participating in the college YMCA in Silliman Hall. He grew in his devotion to missionary work through the Y.[11] His classmates appointed him in 1892 as a delegate to the State Convention held at Auburn.[12] He attended the July 1893 regional conference at Northfield, Massachusetts.[13] He reported on this last conference at a union service of Christian Endeavor Societies of the Methodist, Baptist, and Presbyterian churches in his hometown.[14] At the July 1894 YMCA conference in Northfield, Massachusetts, he signed a "student volunteer" pledge card to become a foreign missionary. He served as the president of the Y his senior year.

Pledge Card[15]

Learning that George signed a Pledge Card brought back memories of me signing a similar pledge card for the Christian Service Corps while a student at Maryville College in the early 1970s. I signed the card around the time I felt the urgency to devote myself to missions. I withdrew from college without telling my parents. When my dad heard what I had done, he called me and told me to reenroll because the world could wait until I finished my education. He had contemplated missionary service twenty years earlier during his last semester in medical school.

After I reenrolled at Maryville, God called me into Christian ministry at the church I attended. Seventeen months later, during my first semester at Gordon-Conwell Theological Seminary, I signed a World Evangelization Decision Card. I marked the box that I did not know if it was God's will to serve overseas, but I was convinced I had a part in God's worldwide agenda.

Dad and Mom volunteered as medical missionaries with the United Presbyterian Church, USA in Embangweni, Malawi, Africa in 1992-94. They could not stop talking about the mission field when they returned. Their legacy there continues to this day.[16]

George practiced a private spiritual life. He made daily time for appointments with God in the solitude of his dormitory room to pray and meditate. He willingly told his fellow students what his allegiance to Jesus Christ meant to him. Anthony Petersen did not consider him a great orator, but when he spoke in Y meetings in Silliman Hall, George spoke with clarity and conviction.

MANDOLIN CLUB, 1894.

George is on the right, back row. Courtesy of Hamilton College Archives.

George joined the Delta Upsilon fraternity like his pastor Rev. Bayless. He served as managing editor of the yearbook, *Hamiltonian*, played the cello in the Bango/Mandolin Club, participated in debates, penned essays, and entered speaking contests.

The Utica *Herald* reported that George and another Mexico student at the college participated in the McKinney Prize Declamation. His sophomore subject was "The Fall of Jerusalem." He gave a commendable effort.[17]

George obtained the first prize in the McKinney Prizes for English essays. His subject "The German of Tacitus and the North American Indians" compared the Roman writer Tacitus' descriptions of the Germans to Native Americans. George spoke with a pleasant eloquence and used many generalizations about both people groups. He highlighted commendable traits, religious heritage, and customs. The purpose of the essay, however, was to show that the Germans advanced by slow degrees till they became a formidable European power. Native Americans, on the other hand, stayed at the same level of development as when they first met Caucasians. They were like the Germans fourteen-hundred years before and were unwilling to assimilate into the American culture because of their ultra-conservativism. The German people, on the other hand, were leaders in progress.[18]

George's mathematical skills led to a second-place prize in the Tompkins Mathematical contest.[19] He earned an Edward Huntington Mathematical Scholarship. The subject for the McKinney prize debate in 1895 was the proposition:

> That the coinage problem can be justly and effectively solved by renouncing the fiction of '16 to 1,' and by coining legal tender silver, always and only upon the basis of the current ratio of its real bullion value to the bullion value of gold.[20]

George courageously opened the debate. He reviewed the history of gold and silver coinage in the country, and other leading nations. He claimed there was not enough gold to put the country on a gold basis, even if such a thing were desirable. Experience showed that a fixed ratio was not possible because of the constant change in the relative value of gold and silver.[21]

George studied geology under the tutelage of Dr. Charles Henry Smyth, Jr., professor of geology and mineralogy. The class made excursions to study local geological sites and minerals. "Our Geology Trip" is a humorous account of a trek to a stream several miles from the college campus. Dr. Smyth and his eight understudies hiked to the stream. As they neared the stream, they encountered a field enclosed by a barbed wire fence. Once inside the field, a bull charged the group. The students ran in different directions to confuse the bull. George and another student ran in one direction praying that the bull would go after the other man.

Everyone got over the fence, but one student's spring suit was ripped apart. Fortunately, he had brought a pair of pajamas that he put on behind a tree. Dr. Smyth landed in mud up to his knees and needed assistance extricating himself out of the bog. Once the class arrived at the stream, a hornet's nest got stirred up and the group had to run for their lives again. Then a thunderstorm arose and drenched them as they raced to a farmhouse to seek shelter.

George and two other students were the most presentable to knock on the door. The pretty farmer's daughter greeted the ragged group and invited them indoors. The farmer's wife served them donuts and apple cider, which apparently was fermented. George suggested the group stay in the house until the storm subsided and then let the farmer take them back to the campus in his wagon. The farmer approved of his idea. On the ride home, they all agreed not to say a word about their disastrous hike. The eight male students made "internal pledges" to revisit the farmhouse to see the pretty young lady, "the queen of donuts and hard cider."[22]

Each student tallied up their losses for the day. George had lost a hat and coat, but did not have to hike the five miles back to campus and expend an unknown amount of energy. If he made an "internal pledge" to revisit the farmer's daughter, this is the closest one gets to his interest in a member of the fairer sex. It is also unimaginable that he partook of hard cider.

George at Hamilton College. Possible graduation photo. Treadwell/Stone collection.

George's discipline and hard work earned him one of the five High Honors in Scholarship awards at graduation. His High Honor Oration subject was *The Causes of the Napoleonic Revival.*[23] He also earned honors in mathematics, rhetoric, and oratory.[24] He was inducted into the Phi Beta Kappa Honor Society.[25] Several graduation week events kept him occupied, including a baseball game between the graduates and undergraduates, a reception at President Stryker's house, commencement, and an alumni dinner. On Sunday June 23, he gave a YMCA report as the outgoing president.[26] He was his parents' first college graduate.

George worked as a farmhand the summer of 1895.[27] This kind of work experience appeared later in the letter he wrote in September 1898 on his journey to Bahrain:

> I did wish that some of my farmer friends around Mexico and Onondaga Hill were with me and we could take a carriage and drive through the country and see everything close by and talk with the people. How each one would enjoy it.[28]

He contrasted how the English and French treated their horses in another letter:

> In London, the whip is not used very much but in Paris they are cracking all the time and tender mercies of the wicked are very cruel. In London they do not use whiffletrees or eveners, except where they hitch one team ahead of another, but fasten the traces to a stationary bar. I think our way is easier for horses.[29]

George learned to harness horses and hitch teams of horses to a carriage or wagon at home. These skills were not the primary ones he needed in the mission field, but they equipped him to handle manual tasks when they needed to be performed.

Phi Beta Kappa Honor Society fob. Douglas Courtright collection.

George looked back on his senior year in his February 1899 letter to President Stryker:

> as sort of a battleground where a few of us struggled to hold the college to honesty in athletic engagement and to lift a little the dead level of religious indifference. I felt I was in a fight all the time & sometimes thought it tough work but now I look at it as the only life to live.[30]

William A. Aikens' fiftieth anniversary graduation letter in 1945 gave a different description:

> No Hamilton man has ever approached the end of his college days without a haunting feeling of regret that the days of intimate companionship, of fun and frolic, are over.[31]

Hamilton companionship, fun, and frolic certainly enriched George's undergraduate days. He matured, opened up, and expanded his horizons during his four years at the college. If he had been alive in 1945, he would have noticed that Mr. Aikens did not mention spiritual or religious vitality. This silence missed George's passion and focus.

Lest we think he did not love Hamilton, he took time out of his busy seminary schedule to attend the Presentation Holiday in the College Chapel on Tuesday, November 16, 1897. This event dedicated the new Root Hall of Science and Benedict Hall of Languages. The chapel interior had been rebuilt too. New York Governor Frank S. Black and Congressman James S. Sherman added dignity to the ceremonies. Hundreds of alumni and friends of the college attended, and George joined them in loudly proclaiming their love for the school.[32]

CHAPTER 3

Ministerial Training at Auburn Seminary

Following success at Hamilton College, George entered Auburn Theological Seminary in September 1895.[1] He received a call from God for vocational ministry and dedicated himself to foreign missionary service. Where this service would take him became the pressing question at seminary. His participation in Christian Endeavor at his home church, with the college YMCA, and attending Y conferences kept him connected to the mission field through literature he read and the speakers he heard.

Auburn was about fifty miles south of Mexico. George's pastor, Rev. George Bayless, a graduate of Hamilton College ('64) and Auburn Seminary ('67), influenced his choice of Auburn. The seminary did not start keeping records of the students' academic standings until 1901, so George's academic achievements are not known.[2]

The seminary was founded in 1818 by the Presbyterian Synod,[3] and the New York Legislature passed the Act of Incorporation on April 4, 1820.[4] The seminary welcomed students from other denominations.[5] Two years before George matriculated, the seminary chose its first president in 1893, then erected the new chapel and lecture rooms in 1894.[6] George appreciated these new facilities. He studied Hebrew, Greek, Old and New Testament, philosophy and theology, principles of Bible interpretation, pastoral theology, sermon preparation, church history, and church government. George lived in Morgan Hall.

Attendance and class size reached their peaks when George entered. His first year, 1895-96, recorded the highest attendance at 123 students. The graduating class of 1897 was the largest with forty-six.[7] He heard guest lecturers such as the Rev. Edward H. Griffin, DD, LLD, Dean of Johns Hopkins University and Professor of Philosophy; the Rev. James S. Dennis, DD, a former missionary in Syria and author of many volumes on Christian Missions; and the Rev. William R. Terrett, DD, Professor of American History at Hamilton College.[8]

The Rev. William H. Mason, a classmate, related that during their first year George sat at his dinner table while Mason and other students jokingly called him "Poor George Stone." With the passing of time, the incongruity of the label revealed that he:

> was rich in everything that made life priceless. He was a Christian of the highest type. The classroom to him was not the place to exhibit any superiority of knowledge, but simply a place in which to learn of Jesus. Any show of self-conceit on the part of a fellow student met his silent but withering rebuke.[9]

Mason saw new richness to George's character each day, which was the subtle charm of George's life. He did not make enemies, but he did not deviate from his simple adherence to what he thought right. "Principle left no place in him for policy." At the end of his seminary career, he did not boast about his missionary plans, yet he "never doubted that God had called him to an important work."[10]

George looked back on his seminary career when he wrote to Hamilton College's President Stryker from Bahrain. In contrast to the college curriculum, Auburn's "life didn't agree with me—it was too easy."[11]

CHAPTER 4

Prepared for the Work of Service

George's practical experience in ministry supported Samuel Zwemer's opinion that he was a man of the Mission's hopes. Academic training prepares a person's mind. Practical training equips a person for service. A major portion of training for ministry is developing one's preaching skills and aptitude.

George's earliest known preaching opportunity occurred on Sunday morning in the Prattham Presbyterian Church, December 29, 1895. Prattham is about two-and-a-half miles east of Mexico. His parents and other relatives attended the service to hear and support him. Butterflies fluttered in George's stomach as he waited to preach, but once he started speaking the word of the Lord, his nerves calmed down and the Spirit empowered his delivery. Mr. Humphries, who also attended the service, reported that George's delivery was very acceptable.[1]

George chose to serve as the student pastor at the Onondaga Hill Presbyterian Church (OHPC) on the west side of Syracuse and approximately twenty-two miles east of Auburn. He became a regular customer of the train to and from OHPC. He brought a youthful energy to the small congregation. This instilled hope in the people for their worshipping community. They served as his real life instructors in human relations, pastoral care, and preparing a diet of nourishing spiritual food in his preaching. The historic church continues to serve the community in the twenty-first century.[2]

Student pastors tend to be younger than the adult membership of churches. This creates a tension for the church and student. Older church members do not think a student pastor is qualified to counsel them because he does not have enough life experiences. On the other hand, the student needs chances to learn from the older adults. George followed the apostle Paul's admonition to the youthful Timothy:

> Don't let anyone look down on you because you are young,
> but set an example for the believers in speech, in life, in love,
> in faith and in purity.[3]

The few church records that exist about George's service with the church are brief. The records respectfully, but incorrectly, identify him as Reverend. The first record states, "May 1896. Rev. George Stone a student of Auburn Theological Seminary began his labors with this church." The records leave the impression that services were not held every week.

George returned to Mexico to preach in his home church on Sunday morning, May 10. He preached a clear and powerful sermon contrasting the lives of Saul, the King, and Saul, the Pharisee. The sermon was "very helpful and suggestive."[4] This summary and assessment suggests his familiarity with the Old and New Testaments and his creativity in correlating the two biblical characters in a purposeful way. The Onondaga Hill church records are devoid of any descriptions of his sermons, pastoral care, or friendships with the people. The summaries of his sermons found in the Mexico *Independent* only give us snippets of the sermons.

George led the evening service at OHPC on Friday, August 28, 1896, in preparation for the observance of the Lord's Supper on Sunday.[5] His presentation was called a preparatory lecture. This type of meeting gave church members the opportunity to examine their lives and make amends, if necessary, so that their partaking of the communion elements on Sunday was with a clean heart. The apostle Paul wrote:

> A man ought to examine himself before he eats the bread and drinks the cup. For anyone who eats and drinks without recognizing the body of the Lord eats and drinks judgment on himself.[6]

George filled the OHPC pulpit very admirably during the summer of 1896.[7] He served the church two years, which were his middle and senior years, respectively, at the seminary.[8] He preached at his home church again on July 12. The sermon text was John 12:24:

> Verily, verily, I say unto you, Except a corn of wheat fall into the ground and die, it abideth alone: but if it die, it bringeth forth much fruit.

He preached in the evening on Romans 1:1-7, holding the attention of his listeners.[9] Later in November, he preached in Osceola, approximately thirty-five miles east of Mexico.[10] He concluded his preaching for the year in both services at the Mexico church on December 27. George's friends were delighted to listen to "his able presentations of the truth."[11]

George closed out 1896 at the second annual "Meet" of the alumni of Mexico Academy on December 31. He used his public speaking skills as the event's toastmaster and:

> grasped the toast fork and with a few well directed remarks, he soon had the slices [of cake] in the hands of most accomplished connoisseurs who served them up after the most approved style.[12]

He preached again at his home church in the evening service on April 4, 1897. He "preached an excellent sermon...and his theme was the value of Christian service."[13] His text was Acts 20:24:

> But none of these things move me, neither count I my life dear unto myself, so that I might finish my course with joy,

and the ministry, which I have received of the Lord Jesus, to testify the gospel of the grace of God.

The text and theme give us another hint that George was thinking about the personal cost of serving the Lord in missionary service. He chose to turn his back on a so-called "better life" to serve God. The ultimate cost of serving Christ might be death.

George participated in the 1897 Memorial Day observances in Onondaga. Since Memorial Day fell on a Sunday, the planning committee scheduled a union service Sunday evening and the Memorial ceremonies Monday morning. Sunday night, Civil War veterans and their friends attended the service hosted by the Methodist Episcopal Church, where George preached the sermon.[14] Monday morning, he and two other ministers gave short addresses followed by reminiscences from veterans. The audience then marched to the cemetery where the concluding ceremony took place.

What did George speak about at these services? His father and uncles did not serve in the military in the Civil War, so he could not tell the audience family war stories. Did he speak of the valuable service rendered by the men who paid the ultimate price in the war? Or the courageous service of the living veterans to emancipate the slaves and preserve the Union? He could have talked about witnessing the dedication of the Civil War monument in his hometown on July 4, 1889.[15]

George continued his ministry at the OHPC into April of 1898. He wrote a brief opinion of the value of his work at the church in a missionary letter:

> When I look back to my seminary days I think that the work at Onondaga Hill was the best part of it as far as preparing me to be a missionary. The preaching and pastoral work I liked and did my best with, and I reap the benefits of it now.[16]

He would agree with the observation Santiago, the shepherd in Paulo Coelho's *The Alchemist*, made when he told Fatima, "Well, usually I learn more from my sheep than from books."[17]

George's older brother Ernest requested his participation in his wedding ceremony on Monday, September 13, 1897, in Meridian about thirty-five miles south of Mexico. He assisted the officiating minister by reading scripture and offering a prayer for the couple in the home of the bride, Jessie Pauline Drew.[18] Ernest and Pauline enjoyed sixty-three years of marriage but did not have any children. The fall semester at Auburn began two days after the wedding.

CHAPTER 5

Clarity about God's Calling

George's third year at Auburn brought clarity to him about God's calling. He volunteered to serve with the Arabian Mission at a crucial time in the Mission's existence. His appointment to the Mission occurred during the time that the Mission's Rev. Peter J. Zwemer came down deathly sick in Muscat, Oman. Peter was the younger brother of Samuel Zwemer. He established the Mission station at Muscat in 1893 and founded the Rescued Slave Boys School in 1896.[1]

Peter left Muscat in the latter part of May 1898 to return to the United States for better medical care. He never recovered and died at the age of thirty on October 18, 1898, in the Presbyterian Hospital in New York City. George's addition as the newest male volunteer encouraged the Mission even more. He was not Peter's replacement, but he became a crucial addition to the staff.

The Arabian Mission was birthed in 1889 at the New Brunswick Theological Seminary in New Jersey. The Seminary was connected to the Reformed (Dutch) Church in America (RCA). The seminary's Dr. John G. Lansing, professor of Old Testament Language and Exegesis, and three students—James Cantine, Samuel Zwemer, and Philip Phelps—joined in the venture. They discussed, prayed, and researched the matter of creating an organization to reach the Muslim world. Through these deliberations, they were led to focus on the Arabian peninsula, the mother land of Islam.

The application to the RCA's Board of Foreign Missions to unite with its foreign mission program was denied due to the Mission Board's financial constraints. The four men decided to organize on their own. The founders picked the name Arabian Mission. Its field would be "Arabia or adjacent coast of Africa."[2] The Mission chose its motto from Genesis 17:18: "Oh that Ismael might live before Thee."

Arabia covers a large expanse of land. It is mentioned several times in the Bible.[3] The northern portion borders what was formerly called Canaan or Palestine. In Galatians 4:25, the Sinai Peninsula is called Arabia. Earlier in this letter, Paul wrote that he went to Arabia from Damascus. Scholars are divided about what region of Arabia he visited. Arabs were present in Jerusalem at Pentecost when the Holy Spirit descended upon the disciples.[4] In 1898, Arabia covered the large peninsula that included Oman on the southeast shore, Aden and Yemen on the southwest shore, Bahrain in the Persian Gulf, and up to Busrah, Iraq.

The seed for Islam arose in Mecca, Arabia, through Muhammad (born circa 570 CE, Common Era), its most revered prophet. According to the Islamic narrative, at the age of forty in 610 CE, Muhammad began to receive revelations and to instruct people. The response to his message and efforts to cleanse Mecca of its idolatry was slow. When hostility arose, he and his followers fled to Yathrib, which is now called Medina, in 622. This event is called the Hegira and is considered the beginning of Islam.

Muhammad led his followers in battle. He was an exceptional military leader and achieved remarkable success in subduing tribal opponents in order to consolidate the gains. After his death in 632, his revelations were collated into the Quran, Islam's most sacred book. The sayings and experiences of Muhammad are contained in the Hadith or Sunnah and a form of analogical reasoning, qiyas.[5]

Islam's simple creed is "There is no God, but God, and Muhammad is the apostle of God." It believes in one God; angels, jinn, and devils; sacred writings; prophets; resurrection of the body; the Day of Judgment; and predestination. The five duties of its followers are: recitation of the creed; stated prayers five times daily; observing the month of fasting, called Ramadan; giving legal alms; and the pilgrimage to Mecca at least once in a person's lifetime.[6]

Rev. James Cantine was the first missionary to depart the US in October 1889. Samuel followed the next year.[7] They chose Busrah, Iraq, for the site of the first Mission station. The second station opened at Manama, Bahrain, and then one opened in Muscat in 1893. The work included evangelism, basic medicine, education, and literature distribution. The Mission became an official organization of the RCA in 1894, four years before George joined it.[8]

Samuel Zwemer and his wife Amy returned to the United States in 1897 for their first furlough. He lectured at colleges and seminaries, spoke at conferences, and in churches. Amy also made many presentations about ministry with Muslim women and children. Rev. Zwemer made appeals for volunteers to join the Arabian Mission. George was the first inquirer to apply and be accepted.[9]

Samuel spoke at the Student Volunteer Movement Convention in Cleveland, Ohio, on February 23-27, 1898. George's seminary friends elected him and twelve other students to attend the convention,[10] "which confirmed him more than ever in his purpose to give his life to the cause of foreign missions."[11] He joined 1,586 other students, while there were a total of 2,221 delegates.[12] It was the largest gathering of Christians he ever attended. He knew he was on to something special when he looked at the huge audience, heard the stirring messages from so many missionary dignitaries, and joined in the singing with so many voices.

George attended Samuel Zwemer's three presentations: "Arabia," "The Problem of Mohammedanism," and "Personal Dealing—The Great Missionary Method."[13] These fifteen-minute presentations gave brief overviews on each topic. The first presentation covered the contemporary condition and beliefs of Islam. In the second one, Zwemer focused on the land of Arabia and its surroundings. The third presentation emphasized the importance of personal relationships with Muslims in sharing the good news of Jesus Christ the Son of God.

George introduced himself to Samuel at the convention, and this started their friendship. Samuel became his mentor in all things Arabian. George had first heard about the needs of Arabia through a former roommate at Hamilton College, who was attending Union Theological Seminary. This friend attended the Eastern District of the American Inter-Seminary Missionary Alliance Conference at New Brunswick, New Jersey, on November 5-7, 1897.[14] He told George about the conference and Arabia. George wrote shortly thereafter for information about the field and then submitted his application. Rev. Dr. Henry Cobb, RCA Foreign Mission Board's Corresponding Secretary, interviewed him. George received his appointment in January.[15] Eight months later, he wrote home while en route to Bahrain:

> I am glad that I can heartily say that I have not for one moment regretted the step I took last January but find an increasing joy in looking forward to the future.[16]

Samuel Tyndale Wilson, Professor of English Language and Literature at Maryville College in Maryville, Tennessee, attended the convention in Cleveland. He gave a report about it at a Bible study after he returned to the college:

> The convention was not a noisy one, but the spirit of the whole convention was a deep consideration of how the missionary question can be solved.[17]

He gave seven ideas that permeated the convention: Christians are Christ's men to do Christ's work; the will of Christ is that the world be evangelized; this evangelization must be speedy; young people must push forward this evangelization; college men are best prepared to lead in this great work; *we* have a special duty to perform in promoting this worldwide enterprise; it is *my* work to help in the evangelization of the world. These ideas energized George before and after the convention.

George became one of thousands of college and seminary students in the 1890s who volunteered to serve overseas. The Student Volunteer Movement (SVM) traces its history back to 1886 at a college conference in Northfield, Massachusetts. The SVM was organized in 1888. The sense of urgency in completing Jesus Christ's Great Commission to go into all the world experienced a fresh and powerful wave of enthusiasm.[18] The SVM, however, was not a missionary sending agency. It was a missionary advocacy organization. The Arabian Mission sent George to Arabia, not the Student Volunteer Movement.

Auburn Seminary students organized a Student Volunteer Band in 1894. It met and prayed regularly for the graduates who were already in the field and those preparing to go. George's classmate H. H. Barstow reported in the first edition of the *Auburn Seminary Review* that fifty-two graduates were already in foreign fields and three were slated to go in 1897.[19] George's seminary friends elected him to attend the SVM Convention. He was a member and treasurer of the Society of Missionary Inquiry in his middle year.[20]

George welcomed Samuel Zwemer to Auburn Seminary during the last semester on Monday, March 28. He gave Zwemer a tour of the lovely campus that showed early signs of spring, introduced him to some of his friends and professors, and showed him his dormitory room. In between these conversations and visits, he asked questions of Zwemer concerning preparations for the mission field. His guest also advised him to contact the RCA headquarters about attending the Foreign Missionary Day at the Annual RCA Convention in Asbury Park, New

Jersey in June. In the evening, George introduced Samuel to the audience before his lecture on missionary service in Bahrain. Zwemer's presentation elicited interest from the students for literature on Arabia that arrived in April for George to distribute.[21]

CHAPTER 6

Preparing for the Mission Field

George requested ordination by the Presbytery of Syracuse.[1] He presented himself as an evangelist and missionary, expecting to go to south Arabia.[2] His pastor, Rev. Bayless, and his uncle, Benjamin Stone, attended the event held in Syracuse on April 11. Rev. Dr. Arthur Y. Brown, DD gave a presentation on Foreign Missions.[3] The Presbytery "confirmed the call I have long felt in my heart from God himself."[4]

The ordination took place at the East Syracuse Presbyterian Church.[5] Rev. Bayless gave the ordination prayer.[6] George officially received the title of "Reverend." Rev. Zwemer later confirmed George's presentation of himself as an evangelist at the ordination examination:

> No one could travel with him and not know he was a fisher of men; yet he was never obtrusive in his methods.[7]

The OHPC records state that the April observance of the Lord's Supper would be postponed so George could officiate at the service on April 17, the Sunday after his ordination. The church people respected him and were proud of their role in his development as a minister of the gospel.

Onondaga Hill Presbyterian Church record pertaining to George's ordination. Used with permission.

After George administered communion on April 17, he regretfully resigned his position with the Onondaga Hill Presbyterian Church.

George spoke in the afternoon at the Oswego County Christian Endeavor Societies Convention in Mexico on Thursday, May 12. His home church hosted the meeting.[8] A former principal at Mexico Academy for six years, Rev. Henry Fancher of Batavia, New York, spoke also. He had left the Academy while George was an Academy student to attend seminary to become a minister.

George's topic "The Mohammedan Problem" covered material about Islam. He used Zwemer's material from the Cleveland Convention in February and added his own perspective to it. He started out on a positive note by telling the audience that Islam held to one great truth, one great God, infinite and controlling, which gave it vitality. This truth pleased his listeners. He went on to explain that this great truth is a "bare belief in a sovereign God; there is no mediator," even though "[Muhammad] is their intercessor." As a result, Islam cannot solve the problem of sin. Islam was a barrier to civilization. He touched on Islam's attitude toward and treatment of women, both of which were bad. He urged his audience to offer their ardent prayers to the work of making Jesus King in Arabia. He devoted the balance of his talk to the Cleveland Convention he attended in February and the thousands of volunteers who were going overseas. His presentation was "an earnest, soul-stirring address, and commanded close attention" from his audience. That he was soon leaving for Arabia gave it added significance.[9]

George spoke in his church in the evening service on May 15. He preached on Acts 5:29, "we ought to obey God rather than man." He was suffering from a severe cold, but "ably presented his theme," and "his earnest, candid, convincing discourse" held the attention of his audience.[10] His parents and home church members saw him in a new light: an ordained minister of the gospel of Jesus Christ. They saw how far he had developed. They accepted his divine authorization to engage in ministry, and they would release him into the Lord's service on the mission field in a mere three months.

George packed his bags, bought a round-trip train ticket, and traveled to Asbury Park, New Jersey, to attend the General Synod of the Reformed Church in America the first week of June. In a five-minute speech on the evening of June 6, he stated:

> I don't know what the Lord is going to do with me in Arabia. I don't know what is ahead. But I do know one thing, I know that the Lord and I have entered into a very clear, definite contract. All of its terms are fully understood by both parties to it. According to those terms He is Master, and I am

not. He has shown me He wants me in Arabia, and so I am going.[11]

George admitted that he had wrestled with the decision to be a missionary before making his commitment, "I tried in every possible way to avoid going to the foreign field, but I had no peace. I go from a sense of obedience."[12]

George shortly before leaving for Arabia. Personal collection.

George's next assignment led him from New Jersey to Clifton Springs, New York, to attend the International Missionary Union's 15th Annual Meeting held June 8-14. He spoke Tuesday night, June 14. A total of thirty missionaries were on the platform. Some had returned from the field. Others, like him, were preparing to go out for the first time. His short presentation included a testimony like the one he had presented at the General Synod meeting the week before. He also covered three points about Arabia that sound very much like Samuel Zwemer's material—Arabia is a land of possibilities, a land of opportunities, and people are not as bigoted as in Turkey. He concluded by stating, "Arabia is promised for Christ, and He will give the victory."[13]

George returned home for a short time and then visited his older brothers, Frederick and Ernest, in Dolgeville, New York. They arranged with their pastor for George to preach at their Presbyterian Church on June 26. He did an admirable job.[14] He brought his brothers up to date on his plans and speaking commitments, and he played with his nephews, Albert and Elmore, who were five and two, respectively.

Three weeks later, on July 18, George took the oath of allegiance to the United States. He received his passport on July 21. He described his occupation as:

> clergyman; that I am about to go abroad temporarily; that I intend to return to the United States in two years & perhaps longer with the purpose of residing and performing the duties of citizenship therein.

He was twenty-four years old, five feet ten inches tall, with blue eyes, dark brown hair, and a dark complexion. His cousin, Edward T. Stone, served as his witness.[15]

George preached in the morning service at the Mexico Methodist Church on Sunday, August 7. He preached strongly to a large congregation from the text, "One thing I know, whereas I was blind, now I see."[16] In the evening, he returned to the Prattham Presbyterian Church and delivered a remarkably interesting sermon.[17] The *Independent* announced that the Young People's Christian Education Society of his home church would give an informal reception for him in the chapel on Friday evening, August 12.

Three young men visited George in Mexico on Monday, August 8: H. C. Suitcher of Princeton Seminary, Joseph Walker Miller of Auburn Seminary,[18] and Professor Thomas G. Burt of Park College, Missouri.[19] The *Independent* did not give the reason for the meeting, but at least two of the visitors were friends. They gave George their blessings for his missionary service, prayed for him, and bid him farewell.

CHAPTER 7

Farewell to Mexico, New York

George's last weekend in Mexico began with the informal reception in the Presbyterian Church's chapel Friday evening sponsored by the Young People's Christian Endeavor Society. The event included instrumental music and a vocal solo. The pleasant affair was tempered by the sadness of his imminent departure.[1] He preached at the church on Sunday morning.

The *Independent* included news that several of George's Presbyterian relatives came to town to honor him: his youngest brother Harry from the Thousand Islands; his cousin Walter C. Stone, editor of the Camden, New York *Advance*; and cousins Junius and Avery Stone of Auburn. A large portion of the Stone family met together for the Sunday worship service.

Sunday evening, a union farewell service included the Baptist and Methodist churches. The service included scripture reading, prayer, songs, and George's interesting talk on Arabia where he anticipated living the next seven years, five years more than he thought when he applied for his passport. He held the attention of the audience and:

> gained the hearty sympathy of all present, as he graphically pictured the need of consecrated Christian workers in that country so long neglected.[2]

Rev. Bayless followed George's talk with some remarks. He read an appreciative letter from Rev. T. H. Myers, PhD, pastor of the Methodist Church, who could not attend. The service concluded with the congregation singing "Blest Be the Tie."[3] George saw many wet eyes. A multitude of handshakes and hugs greeted him at the church doors. It was his last full day in Mexico.

George's parents, George W. and Sophie, were sixty-two and fifty-eight years old, respectively. They were proud of him and fearful for him. They did not know what the future held for him. Like other parents, they imagined the worst while they also celebrated the momentous time in their son's life.

Mr. and Mrs. Stone became empty nesters. Their oldest son Frederick left Mexico in 1895 to open a business in Dolgeville, New York. Son Ernest became a partner with Frederick in Dolgeville in 1897. Harry entered Auburn Seminary a month after George's departure. Every parent has a perspective on an adult child's departure as part of the maturation process. The grown child needs to leave. The parents must let them go. The Stones experienced these thoughts and the conflicting emotions.

George and his mother completed their packing for Monday's departure. Mr. Stone stayed in Mexico while Mrs. Stone accompanied George to New York City.[4] Mr. Stone and Harry took them to the Mexico train station and helped them unload their baggage. George's cousin, Edward Stone, joined them at the station and presented to him a purse containing nearly $100 donated by friends as a "token of their love and sympathy in his work."[5] One hundred dollars is equivalent to $3,138 in today's money.[6] Mr. and Mrs. Stone, George, and Harry said their goodbyes, and then Sophie and George boarded the train. They waved to the family from their seats as the whistle blew and the engineer pushed the throttle to start the train on its way.

Mr. Humphries wrote:

> He carries with him to that distant land a spirit of zeal, of consecration, of self-sacrifice and love that is beautiful and, with perfect trust and confidence in his Commander, goes forth to conquer 'in His name.' The love, sympathy, and prayers of all the Christian people here will follow him and all trust that he will be abundantly blessed in his labors.[7]

Mrs. Stone and George fell asleep on the train after such a busy and eventful weekend. When they arrived in New York City at 6 p.m., they hired a ride to the hotel to join Samuel, Amy, and Katarina Zwemer and the other recruit, Ms. Margaret Rice.[8] On Wednesday, they all traveled to the wharf where the HMS *Majestic* awaited them. Mrs. Stone gave her son goodbye kisses, hugs, and words of enduring love that he cherished in the months to come. He boarded the ship with the Zwemers and Ms. Rice, along with all the other passengers. He turned back and looked for his mother one more time. When their eyes met, he waved to her standing on the wharf. They did not know it would be their last glimpse of each other.

The *Majestic* departed Wednesday night, August 17, bound for Liverpool, England.[9] Samuel's brother and missionary partner, Peter Zwemer, was still a patient at the Presbyterian Hospital in the city. George did not mention visiting Peter at the hospital. Mrs. Stone took advantage of her proximity to Dolgeville and visited her sons Frederick and Ernest and her grandsons.[10] She then returned to the arms of her husband in Mexico.

Mr. Humphries kept George's travel news and missionary service alive in Mexico by printing excerpts from his letters. He fulfilled his own words that "all the Christian people here will follow him." Each excerpt appeared several weeks after they were written because mail traveled slowly. For example, his first letter dated August 25 appeared in the

Mexico *Independent* on September 21. Many readers talked to Mr. and Mrs. Stone about the excerpts, told them they were praying for their son, asked if they had received any more news, or asked about things they did not understand in the letters. George was Mexico's son too.

PART II

JOURNEY TO ARABIA

CHAPTER 8

A *Majestic* Trip to Great Britain

At the beginning of 1898, the United States shifted gears into an international engagement with Spain. Tensions between the two countries turned into the Spanish-American War. The *USS Maine* sank from an explosion in Cuba's Havana Harbor on February 15. The war started later in the year, but the sinking of the *Maine* stirred up nationalism to a fever pitch. Investigations into the sinking produced conflicting conclusions about the cause. Before the year ended, the United States' victory in the short war gave it possession of the Spanish colonies of Guam and Puerto Rico. The United States also paid twenty-million dollars for the Philippines. It emerged as an international colonial power, forcing the country to play an increased role in international politics.[1]

The war erupted at a time when the United States had sufficiently recovered from the Civil War to turn its attention from itself and to look outward to the rest of the world. Despite the reversals on implementing and protecting the rights of the freed slaves, the nation regained confidence about itself with industrialization, an influx of immigrants, and technological advances that even Mexico, New York, started to enjoy. The number of states admitted to the Union increased by eight during George's lifetime: Colorado in 1876; North Dakota, South Dakota, Montana, and Washington in 1889; Idaho and Wyoming in 1890; and Utah, which became the forty-fifth state, in 1896.

President William McKinley's 1898 Thanksgiving Proclamation conveyed an upbeat tone:

> Few years in our history have afforded such cause for thanksgiving as this. We have been blessed by abundant harvests; our trade and commerce have wonderfully increased; our public credit has been improved and strengthened; all sections of our common country have been brought together and knitted into closer bonds of national purpose and unity.[2]

He tempered these thoughts by acknowledging that the brief, victorious war marred the year, and the loss of lives grieved the nation.[3] His generalizations about how good the year had been ignored the racial tensions, such as in South Carolina and Mississippi, where Whites and Blacks had clashed, and many people were killed. Citizens in both states anticipated more trouble.[4]

The Christian church in the United States and in Europe experienced an explosion of interest in and endeavors to spread the good news of Jesus Christ worldwide in the latter part of the nineteenth century. Bible societies, missionary organizations, and denominational outreach expanded rapidly. The merging of imperialism and mission outreach created problems. The combination of imperialism and missionary work created confusion about what the missionary enterprise was attempting to do. Many Western Christians considered themselves more advanced and better intellectually and culturally than the people they went to with the good news.[5]

George chose to get involved in international service too. He grew up when development, expansion, and optimism permeated much of the country and missionary efforts. His home church had introduced him to home and foreign missions. George's mother served with the church's large and active Women's Foreign Missionary Society.[6] The church's foreign missions offerings often exceeded the home missions offering in the 1880s.[7] Missions was not foreign to George when he embarked on his journey to Arabia. International travel, however, was foreign to him.

George and his mother gazed in amazement at the huge RMS *Majestic* on August 17 before he boarded the ship set to sail to Liverpool, England. The *Majestic* was eight years old. It was a steamship with three masts, two tall ones and a shorter one at the stern. It had two funnels located between the two tall masts. In 1891, it had captured the Blue Riband (Ribbon) for the fastest westbound trip, but it had lost the Riband two weeks later to another ship. The *Majestic* could accommodate 1,490 passengers. The Zwemer traveling party occupied second-class cabins that accommodated 190 passengers. The voyage was delightful because the Atlantic was extremely calm. The distinguished captain of the ship was Edward John Smith, who later became the one and only captain of the *Titanic*.[8]

George's letters to his parents cover three phases in his short missionary career. The letters from late August to mid-October cover his journey to Bahrain. The late October to mid-February letters introduce readers to his life in Bahrain. The final collection of letters reports on his transfer to and life in Muscat, Oman, to oversee the Mission station. His letters reveal his knowledge, passion, humor, wit, and theological views, and the challenges he faced. They transport the reader from his central New York culture through several other cultures to the Muslim culture of the Persian Gulf region. They also reveal aspects of his character, calling, and courage.

George's excitement that his journey to the mission field had begun was tempered by leaving his family and friends behind. The trip to Bahrain was a long one. They sailed to Liverpool with a stop at Queenstown in Cork, Ireland. They took the train from Liverpool to London and lodged at the North Africa Mission facility in Barking, east of London. They sailed to France, visited Paris, and traveled to Marseilles where they boarded their next ship. They passed by Italy and through the Suez Canal to India and arrived in Bahrain in October.

George's five senses experienced innumerable stimulations during the long trip. Sight, sound, smell, taste, and touch permeate his letters. These letters are the window to peer into his mind and heart in a way not otherwise available to us, except for a few quotations found elsewhere.

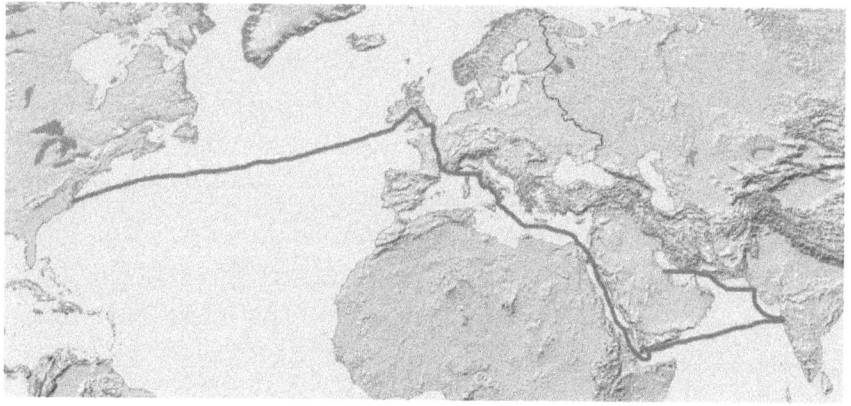

Route to Bahrain[9]

He wrote his first letter aboard the *Majestic*. The brief extract of this letter in the Mexico *Independent* is devoted to the worship services he attended or participated in with Samuel and others on Sunday, August 21. The extract did not include any description of his room or the ship. First and second-class areas hosted morning worship services. George, the Zwemers, and Margaret attended the morning service in their second-class area. The chief steward led the service in which he read the Church of England liturgy. It did not include a sermon, which was expected by George. He and Samuel participated in a 5:00 p.m. service in the steerage. A Mr. Lindale spoke and captivated his audience. He was traveling from Moody Bible Institute in Chicago to South Africa.

Later in the evening, George and Samuel organized their own service in the second-class cabin saloon. The advertisement for the service stated that George would preside. The well-attended service featured Zwemer speaking on "Ten Years in Arabia" and a Rev. W. Cliff on "Ten Years

Among the Red Skins." Since no one in the audience accepted the invitation to play the piano, George accompanied the singing. The audience was intrigued by Samuel and Rev. Cliff's presentations. Sunday closed in a profitable way for George.[10]

The second letter covered the stops at Queenstown, Cork, Ireland, and Liverpool, England, traveling to London, arrival in Barking, and a tour of London on August 25. George roomed at the North Africa Mission (NAM) training school:

> Here I am at last, up in a sort of an attic chamber at the table before a dormer window, with a little bug of a light, in a town of 17,000.... This North Africa Mission is undenominational and works for [Muslims] in North Africa.[11]

Barking is east of the East End, about eight miles from downtown London. Wealthy people resided in London's West End and the poor lived in the East End. The Mission's location allowed it to work among the poor.

George got exasperated with the trip from London to Barking:

> We could get only the laziest sort of idea where the place was from Mr. Zwemer and spent three hours getting across London. We could have come nearly all the way by the underground railroad, if we had been directed right.[12]

Welcome to inadequate communication, incomplete directions, and international travel!

Samuel, Amy, and Katarina stayed in London until Saturday. On Friday, George toured London with Elliot Glenny, a very bright and gentlemanly young man and the son of the NAM's Honorary Secretary, Mr. Edward Henry Glenny.[13] Margaret remained in Barking. She was engaged to the Rev. Frederick J. Barny, another Arabian Mission missionary, who was already in the mission field.

George and Elliot traveled by rail to Fenchurch Street and walked through Lombard Street, the great banking center, to the little square with the Bank of England and the Mansion House. These buildings were located at the intersection of Lombard, Cornhill, and Mansion House Place. Both were fine buildings, but all the buildings in the city were discolored by pollution. The Mansion House was the official residence of the Mayor of London.

They hopped on a three-horse-drawn, double-decker bus called an omnibus. They paid for cheaper seats on the upper deck that gave them a panoramic view.[14] They passed St. Paul's Cathedral:

> a noble structure indeed, but whose beauty is hid by the buildings about it. The streets are narrow, with little alleys just wide enough for a wagon, running off at every angle in the most crazy freedom.[15]

They turned down Fleet Street, lined with the great newspaper offices. Fleet Street connected to the Strand, passing Temple Bar. The Temple Bar was the principal west entrance to the city of London from Westminster. Bar referred to a gate erected across a street or road. George explained that the Temple Bar, according to ancient tradition, could not be passed by Queen Elizabeth I without permission from the Lord Mayor. The Bar was removed in 1878 and rebuilt elsewhere. George saw the Temple Bar monument that was erected in 1880.[16]

They arrived at Trafalgar Square and viewed what he called the Nelson Monument. Its official name is the Nelson Column. It was erected in 1843 with additions made in 1867.[17] They journeyed through Whitehall:

> where the Horse Guards are stationed, each in a little gateway, and neither horse nor man seems to move an eyelid. It seems odd to meet soldiers everywhere, in every sort of gay uniform and odd little caps. The scarlet coats are very conspicuous. It

is a constant reminder that we are not in pacific America, near the storm centre of the world.[18]

How pacific was the United States? The Spanish-American War was fought in April to August. Thirty-five years earlier, the nation had battled over its unity in the Civil War. The country endured numerous wars with Native Americans during George's lifetime.

The two young men exited the bus and walked across Parliament Square where three months earlier Prince Albert of Wales and the great men of England marched to honor the former Prime Minister, William E. Gladstone, who had died May 28, 1898. Statues of distinguished statesmen were located at all the corners. George saw statues of Lord Palmerston, Lord Darby, Lord Beaconsfield, and others.[19]

They hurried to Westminster Abbey and saw more monuments to the great men and women of England. George explained, "I have had so little opportunity before to see anything of the kind that I have no standard to go by, but the statuary seemed wonderful...."[20] He marveled at the sculpture named Death:

> a skeleton, partially concealed in a mantle, is emerging from a tomb, and has poised his dart to strike a woman, while a man, who holds her with one arm, tries to ward off the blow with the other.[21]

The sculpted man and woman were Joseph Nightingale and his wife Lady Elizabeth. George gave an assessment of the symbolism in the sculpture:

> Such a marble speaks at one glance a whole volume in the great tragedy of human life; and yet after all it is but from the human standpoint unaided by the Christian hope, for ever since Christ left Joseph's tomb Death hast lost his power, and man and woman sundered here may meet again in the glorious presence of God himself.[22]

The stop at Westminster Abbey allowed George to visit David Livingstone's memorial. Livingstone had died twenty-five years earlier in May 1873:

> I was glad that I could stand by the grave of Livingstone, the missionary explorer, who all England delighted to honor, and read the words which tell of his great deeds for God and think how every day that life is still speaking, and how many a heart is strengthened to live nobler as it reads of a man who staked all for others....[23]

Like other tourists, George enjoyed some tea at a little restaurant before they boarded a river steamer for a cruise on the River Thames that took them almost to London Bridge. He and Elliot got off the boat and walked to St. Paul's Cathedral, which was larger and grander than Westminster Abbey, but not necessarily more beautiful. Upon entering the cathedral, they stood under its dome and looked up. George thought about church architecture and how it served the purpose of filling one's eyes with beauty:

> As you stand under the dome and look up into that wonderful structure, which seems to rest so lightly upon its massive supports, and then turn your eyes to the apse in front of you and the altar at the end, it certainly is very beautiful.[24]

They arrived in time to observe the 4 p.m. service from the rear of the sanctuary. They weren't able to understand the words:

> but the roll of the great organ and the singing of the male choir was grand.... Sometimes it seemed as though an invisible choir were answering from somewhere up in the high-vaulted roof, and then the sounds would melt away as though they had returned to the skies. I can't describe the effect, but as an Irishman might express it, 'The best sight of the day was the chanting in St. Paul's.'[25]

The young men toured the cathedral after the service, admiring the many sculptures, mostly in honor of great military and naval heroes who died in battle. He was impressed with:

> the great part which the navy has played in the history of England, and to-day it is the glory of the Englishman, and he cares not how much it may cost but Britannia must continue to rule the waves.[26]

General Charles Gordon's Tomb and its memorial tribute impressed him:

> As I remember it, it described him as a man who 'gave his strength to the weak, his substance to the poor, his sympathies to the suffering, and his heart to God,' and I thought to myself, how could the noblest ideal of life be better expressed and in fewer words?[27]

They paid sixpence to walk up the 257 steps inside the dome and into the Whispering Gallery. They visited the gallery first. George explained:

> as we stood in one side of the dome, 112 feet across, and put one ear to the wall we could hear distinctly as the attendant repeated his stereotyped description of St. Paul on the other side.[28]

The Whispering Gallery has been called "the greatest 'accidental' manmade tourist attraction in London, if not the world."[29]

They climbed a winding staircase to the outside gallery above the dome. Haze marred the visibility. Looking east, they saw Tower Bridge; to the south the Crystal Palace; to the north Newgate Prison; and the River Thames flowed from west to east to their south.

The tour ended after George and Elliot walked through Cheapside, an enormously popular shopping district, and sipped tea at 6 p.m.[30]

They arrived back at NAM in Barking about 7 p.m. George thoroughly enjoyable the afternoon.

George then switched gears in his letter and gave more information about the voyage to Liverpool. They had sailed along the southern coast of Ireland on Tuesday evening, August 23 and stopped at Queenstown, Cork, Ireland. The cliffs and the hills were:

> touched with the setting sun, and the little farms on the hillside, and apparently no trees, while all about us were the little fishing boats with their brown-black sails, and now and then a lighthouse perched on some picturesque rocky islet.[31]

Two tenders met the *Majestic* to take off passengers and baggage. George bought Cork newspapers to catch up on the news. The United States was still undamaged in spite of the fact that they, as representatives of the Arabian Mission, had been away six days. After a short delay, the *Majestic* set sail again.

In the morning, the *Majestic* passed by Holyhead, Wales, which is situated on Holy Island. Sailing vessels headed for Liverpool, England, from Cork sail around Holy Island and then east to enter Liverpool's harbor. The *Majestic* reached Liverpool at noon on Wednesday, August 24. George's party hired a cab to transport them to the train station. George and Samuel sat on the seat with the driver:

> He was a good-natured individual and calmly assured us that no one could lie like the Americans. He was not influenced by the recent revelations of Spanish ability in that direction.[32]

The train ride to London brought comparisons to George's mind. The English rail cars were smaller and gave a much smoother ride than American rails:

> you go over a railroad bed which is not equaled in America and with none of that jolting in starting and stopping to

which our engineers are wont to treat us…I don't know when
I have enjoyed a railroad ride so well.[33]

The immaculate countryside impressed him. His farming experience back home gave him a keen eye:

> The country seemed like a well-kept park or, when planted, like a garden…. I took solid comfort looking at those grain fields and seeing how well farming could be done when people know how and take pride in doing it well.[34]

He added some humor that the folks back home appreciated:

> Nothing is like America, except advertisements of Pear's Soap, Millen's Food and Carter's Little Liver Pills. I thought I had left them behind when I boarded the Majestic, but now I expect when I land in Bahrain to see on every mud hut along the shore, 'Good morning, have you used Pear's Soap?' or 'Carter's Little Liver Pills.'[35]

Another bit of humor came near the end of his letter:

> At the railroad station I saw a sign… 'plants for hire and flowers,' and I didn't know but what I should find some man who wanted to rent me a hill of potatoes, but none such appeared.[36]

The Zwemers arrived in Barking on Saturday. Samuel preached in the Sunday morning service. George preached in the evening service on Acts 5:29 "we must obey God rather than men." This was the same text for the sermon at his home church on May 15. A good sermon is always worth repeating when the opportunity arises. The Lord's Supper was observed after each service. He added:

> It was a very helpful day and the very simplicity of it all made it seem more like what gatherings of the early Christians must

have been. Some of the hymns were sung to old fashioned English tunes such as I never heard before.[37]

On Monday morning, Samuel returned to London to take care of business that included visiting the office of Thomas Cook & Son. This company arranged national and international travel and hospitality.[38] George met him there at 2 p.m. Together, they visited the Bible House of the British and Foreign Bible Society at 146 Queen Victoria Street. They viewed hundreds of Bibles in nearly as many languages, learned that the Society shipped about six thousand Bibles daily, and saw specimens of all kinds of Bibles. They saw the smallest Bible, which was about two inches square, and the great Dutch Bible, nearly a foot thick. The two book lovers then searched the bookstores for books on Arabia, Arabic, and Islam.

Elliott, George, and Margaret toured London on Tuesday. They visited the Tower of London, the four-year-old Tower Bridge, Westminster Abbey, South Kensington Museum, Hyde Park, the Zoological Gardens, and Madame Tussauds. The Tower Bridge was much smaller than the Brooklyn Bridge. The skeletons of a mammoth and giant sloth at the South Kensington Museum made a big impression, but their tourist eyes began to ache from seeing so many displays. Hyde Park is the site of the Albert Memorial built in memory of Queen Victoria's husband Prince Albert. They saw an amazing collection of wax figures at Madame Tussauds where the tour ended:

> At this place we saw everything, and it was nearly 9 o'clock when we started for home, having put in 12 hours of sight seeing.[39]

Samuel commissioned George to write a letter to Dr. Cobb for the whole traveling party. Their hosts, the Glennys, were earnest, practical Christians, which made him happier to stay at the Mission than in London at a boarding house or hotel. Rev. Zwemer learned more about their tickets to Karachi, India (Pakistan, now) and of a quarantine in Bombay (Mumbai) due to the bubonic plague. In closing, George wrote:

> I want to thank you personally for your kind words of instruction and I recognize their justice. With God's help I mean to make the most of my life for Him and I wish to be willing to abide by what the experience of others have found to be wisdom. When there is so much at stake I feel I have no right to be a fool.[40]

George and Margaret returned to London to join the Zwemers on Wednesday morning. The group took Margaret to visit St. Paul's Cathedral. Then they hopped on a train to visit Major General Felix Thackeray Haig (1827-1901) and his wife Christian Anne Haig in Nutfield, about thirty miles south of London. The Haigs lived in a little country place where they were quietly spending their later years. George described them as a fine old couple who warmly received them for an overnight visit. A well-kept garden with gravel walks surrounded the house.

General Haig served as a British military engineer in India rising from the rank of lieutenant to major general. He traveled widely and actively served Jesus Christ. He visited the United States in the 1850s when the Erie Canal was in its prime. He published his observations in *Notes on the River Navigations of North America* in 1863. Haig's tour in the United States had coincided with his engineering work in India. He built the Gunnaram Aqueduct over a branch of the Godavari River to Nagaram Island.[41] George and Samuel updated him on the great commerce conducted on the Great Lakes.

General Haig toured the Arabian coast in 1886. Samuel wrote in a memorial tribute that the general had been the originator of nearly every effort that had been put forward to preach the gospel in Arabia.[42] Haig retired and served as an honorary trustee of the Arabian Mission until his death. He wrote a brief pamphlet, *Modern-Christian Missions in Arabia*, that included information about the Arabian Mission.⁴³ The pioneering work General Haig conducted in prayer, advocacy, and action impacted his visitors.⁴⁴ They bid the Haigs farewell and returned to Barking the next day, September 1, George's twenty-fifth birthday.

Mrs. Amy Zwemer and daughter Katarina stayed overnight in London on Thursday. Samuel returned to London to pick them up while George and Margaret had the pleasure of attending the NAM's Arabic class. NAM required missionary candidates to study Arabic for a year at the Mission school before heading to the field. He knew the alphabet, but he saw wisdom in their policy:

> This saves time on the field and would be a fine thing for our Mission if we could do the same, but we have too few candidates at present. There has been too many other things to do to study much. I shall be glad to start in again next Monday and feel that I am getting nearer Arabia.⁴⁵

A River Thames boat tour occurred on Saturday, September 3.⁴⁶ The tour group included an unidentified number of children connected to NAM. The boat left London and traveled west to the Kew Botanical Gardens in Richmond. George supposed they had passed over the rowing course for the Henley Royal Regatta at Henley-on-Thames, but it was located farther west of London.⁴⁷ The heat bothered him, but the children enjoyed the boat ride. He reflected on how Lake Ontario's beautiful, clear water contrasted with the muddy Thames.

George and his traveling companions prepared for the next leg of their trip when they arrived back in Barking. He looked forward to visiting Paris and Marseilles, France. Then his party would travel by steamer for another 4,000 or 5,000 miles to Bahrain. How he longed for news from home once more.

CHAPTER 9

La Belle France

George's party traveled to the southeast coast of England to catch their boat at Dover. They crossed the English channel to Calais, France:

> Here we are in la belle France—the land of corn and wine and where it is taken for granted that you drink the latter, and the only question is whether it will be white or red wine.[1]

The very noisy train ride from Calais to Paris forced them to shout to each other when talking. Amy, Margaret, and Katarina shared a compartment with three Catholic priests. George and Samuel divided their time between the women's compartment and standing in the corridor observing the scenery. He thought the French countryside with large fields and less population looked more like America's than England's did. Peasants were hard at work with the grain harvesting. Men and women were binding the sheaves. Seeing women in the fields hoeing, weeding, and carrying heavy bundles did not seem right to George.

The tired and dirty party arrived in Paris Monday evening at the Hotel Magenta on Magenta Street in the Tenth District. Amy, Margaret, and Katarina settled in their hotel rooms while the two men went out to buy a takeout supper to eat at the hotel. Paris gave George a better impression than London had. The shop windows were less crowded with merchandise and the advertising was not as profuse as in London. Paris, however, was home to the worst horses of any place he had seen.

George and Samuel visited Notre Dame Cathedral on the southeastern end of Île de la Cité, or city island, in the Seine River. They spent about a half hour at the cathedral. George thought it more beautiful than either St. Paul or Westminster Abbey. The exterior was cleaner than the London buildings were. The bishops wore beautiful vestments with jewels, gold, silver, and precious stones. Priests were:

> chanting away monotonously masses for the dead, and we thought how far these people have gone from the simple teachings of Jesus and how little sympathy He must have for all the nonsense and frippery of the priesthood and ceremonials of Continental Romanism.[2]

They walked from the cathedral to visit the Louvre Museum in the afternoon. Only a small portion of the art works were seen in the hour or so that the men were there. George had read about or seen magazine photographs of the famous paintings in the museum:

> Raphael, Correggio, Murillo and Millet, to say nothing of the others who are not so noted.... As it was I received a confused impression of a thousand masterpieces. Classical mythology and Bible scenes furnished the subject for most of them.[3]

One painting pertaining to Arabia caught George's attention:

> It was entitled 'Pilgrims Going to Mecca,' and represented a caravan crossing the desert at midday. The light effect is so realistic that you could almost feel the scorching heat.[4]

The tour concluded after the men enjoyed a ride along the Champs-Élysées to the Arc de Triomphe and then back to the hotel. The afternoon was hot. George did not mention seeing the Eiffel Tower, which was nine years old and would have been visible. He took pride in his college French that:

has stood me in good stead as, though I can say only a few words, I can read almost everything. Mr. Zwemer can talk more than I can, and between us we get along first-rate.[5]

He made another comparison:

> One thing is certain, we have left Protestant Christianity behind, at least we have no more of the Christian fellowship which…made our stay in England so delightful. Henceforth everything begins to shade, down more and more to the heathen standards of living, and we will soon be where the darkness can be felt. A thin glamor of civilization seems to hide it here but that will not last.[6]

The traveling party boarded the train Wednesday morning for the thirteen-hour ride to Marseilles in southern France. The cloudless, sunny day was prettier than they were when they arrived dirty and tired. The dirt came from the compressed blocks of coal dust mixed with tar used for fuel. It was economical, but the burning blocks produced a nasty soot that a person did not feel in contrast to the cinders produced on American trains. After a few hours on the train, George was transformed with a fine Ethiopian complexion.

The train traveled through the beautiful Fountainebleau forest that had once been the royal preserve. It crossed the broad plains of central France where French farmers lived in villages and not in separate homesteads as American farmers did. South of Lyons was located a multitude of mulberry trees on which silkworms were grown and harvested. George thought the Rhone River valley was the most beautiful region in France. The dirty and tired travelers arrived in Marseilles late at night, which meant his best view of the city and harbor occurred as their steamer departed.

George and his friends boarded the SS *Peninsular* at 3 a.m. Thursday and found their luggage in good order. Their cabins were large. He roomed with three men. Two of them were bound for Mumbai (Bombay), India, and the third man was a young British Navy sailor going to Aden on the southwest coast of Arabia. The food tasted better than on the *Majestic*, though he did not have any complaints about its food.

CHAPTER 10

Introduction to the Orient

Boarding the *Peninsular*, George began his introduction to the Orient, by which he meant the Middle East. The officers, stewards, and a few sailors were English, but the remainder of the crew was composed of Goanese and Lascars from India[1] and Africans who escaped from slavery at Muscat.[2] They spoke an Arabic dialect that Samuel could comprehend enough to converse with them. The Lascars were dressed in white trousers, blue frocks reaching to the knees, and red handkerchiefs around their waists. They wore little red caps wound around with another red handkerchief. The other passengers included a British-educated Persian who was married to an Englishwoman. He was an intelligent and courteous man from Mumbai (Bombay). The diverse company on the ship served as a foretaste of the world George would see in the coming days.

The *Peninsular* departed Marseilles at 4 p.m. Thursday, September 8, bound for Port Said in Egypt. The Mediterranean Sea was calm, and the temperature was about 85° Fahrenheit. Friday morning, they passed through the Strait of Bonifacio between Sardinia and Corsica. A child died Friday night and was buried at sea. Saturday morning, they passed the Lipari Islands, and by noon, they entered the Straits of Messina, which separate Sicily from Italy's mainland.

George reflected on the Apostle Paul's journey two millenniums earlier when he visited Syracuse on Sicily and Rhegium on the mainland:

> It requires a big stretch of the imagination to change this quiet sea into a stormy sea, and our powerful steamer into an old Roman wheat ship, and its banks of oars driven at the mercy of the wind and waves. A great deal of history has been made on and about these waters. It has been the highway for armies, commerce and messengers of the Cross.³

The ship's captain read the Anglican worship service Sunday morning in the first-class saloon. Sunday evening entertainment included a sacred concert. George engaged a Persian gentleman in several conversations on the trip. The man was not well-informed about his religion's teachings and he had doubts about the future life.

George could eat six times a day, but he relied on four meals. Stewards served tea and crackers before breakfast and crackers and cheese at 9 p.m.:

> tea is the only thing we have which corresponds to Mark Twain's description of steamer fare, that 'it was furnished by the Deity and cooked by the devil.'⁴

To fill the time between the meals, George and his friends paced the deck and sat in the lounge chairs they bought in Marseilles. They read, slept, and played with baby Katarina. Time went by quickly. The crew and other passengers warned George that hotter temperatures awaited him in the Red Sea.

In a quiet moment, George remembered that colleges and seminaries were opening in the United States:

> It seems strange that I am all through with those things. I am still a student notwithstanding. I am whacking away at the Arabic and [Samuel] thinks I make commendable progress. It is slow enough at best. It will help me to begin in earnest at Bahrain.⁵

The *Peninsular* arrived in Port Said Monday evening, September 12. George had not seen a city like Port Said before, so he did not know how to describe it. The city was established in 1859 on the shore of the Mediterranean Sea to house the builders of the canal.[6] The city was the meeting place of all nationalities. The Bible was distributed in sixty languages by the British and Foreign Bible Society. The office was located opposite the public gardens in the Place de Lesseps.[7] The port was:

> one of the greatest, if not the greatest coaling stations in the world. The work is done by Arabs, who carry the coal in baskets from the coal scows, which are towed alongside. They wear superfluous clothing and [are] covered with coal dust and yelling like demons all the time, as they run up and down the inclines, you wonder whether they can be human beings.[8]

The *Peninsular* anchored offshore, so a boat taxi took them to land at 10 a.m. A threepence tax was paid to the local sheikh. George learned immediately how stifling hot the sun was in Egypt. The traveling party visited the office of Thomas Cook & Son to check on mail. Leaving the women at the office, George and Samuel hired a two-horse cart for an hour tour. They purchased pith hats to protect themselves from the blazing sun. George also purchased a thin cotton jacket. Samuel's knowledge of Arabic made it easy to find out anything they wanted to know. In the Arab district, they visited a small mosque. They donned galoshes to cover their feet so that as non-Muslims they would not defile the mosque. It was nearly impossible to keep the galoshes on; George was sure they left some defilement in the holy place.

A group of boys sat with their teacher in the mosque. Samuel impressed the students and teacher by reciting two chapters of the Quran and reading other portions. Leaving the mosque, the two tourists passed by the little box-like business shops that were open to the street with men working at their trades. An Arab school was also located among the shops:

It would be a hopeless task in such a place to try to teach American boys, and as the boys watched us as long as we were in sight, I doubt if they make very much progress.[9]

The two men rejoined the women at the Thomas Cook office but then went back out again on foot to visit the Bible Society and other shops. They were the only non-Arabs on one street where women sold their grapes. They were so dirty that George and Samuel did not dare to buy anything. Almost all the people had eye troubles caused by blowing sand, glare of the sun, flies, or a combination of all of these.

The unexpected longer stay at Port Said gave George time to have:

a good look at the sort of life I shall live hereafter and can brace myself for the future. Miss Rice thought the prospect pretty dubious, but I am sure I shall enjoy it when I can jabber with them a little, for they seem to be a friendly people, and a little dust won't kill me.[10]

George and his friends returned to the *Peninsular* and entered the Suez Canal during the night. The canal passed through barren wasteland, and the only interesting things George saw were camels and naked Bedouin boys running along the canal begging for food. The trip took sixteen hours at five miles an hour. The south end of the canal opened to the Red Sea, but George did not see any redness, just blue water. A strong wind on the first day provided relief, but after that just heat.

The cotton jacket George purchased in Port Said came in handy to protect him from the intense sunlight. He got even more comfortable by discarding his underwear. One night, he took his rug out on the hurricane deck and slept there. He did not find the heat as bad as he expected, but other passengers familiar with the region said they had never found it hotter. George found the heat comparable to the hot spells in his hometown.

The regular onboard worship service was omitted on Sunday, so George's group and other people organized an impromptu service. Samuel spoke, and a lady led the singing with a violin. George informed his parents they were all doing well.

The journey on the Red Sea took George the closest that he would ever be to the two most holy sites in Islam, Mecca and Medina. These cities are located inland on the east side of the sea. He could not see them from the deck of the steamer.

The next stop on Sunday night at the city of Aden was short. The city is situated on a peninsula on the southern coast of Yemen. It served as a coaling station for British shipping since the beginning of the nineteenth century. It was nicknamed "Coalhole of the East."[11] The *Peninsular* departed for Mumbai (Bombay) shortly after midnight. George tolerated the corkscrew motion of the boat on Monday, but the others in his group were bothered by terrible seasickness. He and Samuel delivered what little food Amy and Margaret wanted to eat to their rooms.

Concerts were held on the ship every few days. Two or three African servant boys sang American songs such as "Daisy Bell (Bicycle Built for Two)" and "Ta-ra-ra Boom-de-ay" in broken English. They had learned the songs at shows and other events while pulling fans called punkahs.[12] An English officer sang, "Little Alabama Coon."[13] Hearing the familiar American songs made George feel closer to home. The songs also led him to ruminate, "If only the Gospel could circulate as easily."[14]

Few passengers showed an interest in religion. One of them thought everyone should live to be happy, and if they had time to be good. George believed many of the passengers would have wanted to get rid of him and his party because they freely talked about their faith with the passengers.

During the day, the ship passed little schools of flying fish. The large ones looked like American chubs with wings. They could fly for dozens of feet without touching the water, or with just their tails, before ascending above the water again. George thought either the red fungus growth in the water or the abundant small jellyfish floating just below the water's surface might have been the origin for the Red Sea's name.[15] Such sights filled up some of the monotony on the steamer along with his Arabic studies. He thought he was slowly getting the idea of the language:

> It is a fine language, and I am sure that I shall enjoy learning it, even though at times it may seem a hopeless task. When I think how long I have spoken, read and studied in English and yet make mistakes I am not surprised that it takes so long to learn Arabic. Mr. Zwemer suggested to-day that I make a vow not to shave until I had learned Arabic. The only trouble with that is, that I might have to carry my whiskers in a basket before the Arabic was conquered.[16]

George assumed while he wrote to his parents they would be attending the church prayer meeting:

> in the place where prayer is wont to be made for the church and the world, and I love to think, too, for 'one who has gone to preach the gospel in foreign lands;' and rest assured that those prayers are heard, and God is working out all things well and will use me in Arabia.[17]

The trip reinforced his decision to serve with the Arabian Mission:

> I am glad that I can heartily say that I have not for one moment regretted the step I took last January but find that an increasing joy in looking forward to the future. I feel sure, too, that you are finding the brighter side, even though you are bearing the heavier load. 'My grace is sufficient for you' is

still true. One thing I am sure need not trouble you. Through all this constant change of food and drink and more or less irregularity of sleep, I have kept perfectly well and as ready for Arabia as when I left Mexico.[18]

George felt sympathy for his parents whom he believed carried the heavier burden. Their mutual assumption was that they would not see each other for several years. The hard task of learning Arabic did not compare to them saying good-bye to the one they loved.

CHAPTER 11

Hello, India

Mumbai (Bombay) and Karachi, India were the next two stops on the journey to Bahrain. British steamers and cargo ships from Hong Kong, Oman, and other nations were docked at the wharfs or moored in Mumbai (Bombay) harbor. Going to shore was restricted due to the bubonic plague ravaging India. Several hundred people were dying each day. The deaths were most prevalent among the poor on account of their living conditions.

George did not leave his ship, but he saw Hindus with their foreheads marked with different signs according to their castes. They wore colorful clothing, what clothing they wore. They labored to transfer the luggage to a much smaller steamer, the *Kola*. Some of George's party's luggage was left at Mumbai (Bombay) but arrived later in Karachi. The matter of tracking and transferring luggage led him to think that if he were to take another long trip, he would ship the luggage separately and simply use a carry-on bag for his personal needs.

The *Kola* rolled on the sea swells, causing seasickness as it sailed for Karachi. George, once again, was spared from the sickness. He enjoyed the smaller vessel better than the larger ones for the officers were more sociable and several of them were Christians. Captain Livingston had served as the captain of the ship the other Arabian Mission co-founder, Rev. James Cantine, had sailed on during his very first trip through the Persian Gulf in 1890. Captain Livingston knew about the Mission and thought it would have been wiser to locate the first station in Bahrain rather than in Busrah, Iraq. Time would tell whether his opinion was the better one.

George befriended another officer. He was the chief engineer, an enormously proud Scottish man by the last name of Mackey. He was a congenial fellow with a knack for a "blarneying" argument that the two men enjoyed back and forth in a big way. But even this officer, like the others, had a grudge against the Persian Gulf because it was hot, humid, and isolated from his understanding of civilization. They did not want to return to the Gulf.

Wherever the travelers stopped, they hoped to find mail waiting for them. Mail call became the happiest moment for the traveling band. The mail clerk on the *Kola* stretched his authority and gave them their mail, which was addressed for Bahrain. George's parents wrote a joint letter dated August 30 that cheered him immensely. They reported that they had adjusted to his departure well. This reminded him of the lovely farewell and the kindnesses of all their friends. He would not have known where to begin in thanking them. In another letter, Jess wrote that people thought of sending him ice cream.[1] George replied:

> I wished for American cream, for in England and on the steamers they make an abominable article. On the *Peninsular* one man suggested that it was flavored with hair oil.[2]

They arrived in Karachi Wednesday morning. The group stayed a week. Karachi was a city of about 117,000 people and included a British garrison. It was divided into three parts: the harbor, the military installation, and the city. They passed through customs without any problems.

Captain Livingston recommended the Northwestern Hotel two or three miles from the harbor. It consisted of what George called low sheds. These sheds had two features for comfortable living in the hot environment—broad verandas to keep the sun out and lattices to let in the breeze. Mosquito netting covered George's bed to protect him from the annoying buzzing insects during the night. One of the sheds was the hotel office. The courtyard contained several varieties of shrubs and trees, including bananas, oranges, acacias, palms, and others he did not know. He thought the food was the best since leaving the United States. The rice and curry were very tasty.

George's party got settled at the hotel. They attempted to visit Rev. M. Ball at the Church Missionary Society office, but he was not there. They visited the zoological gardens on their return to the Northwestern.[3] When Rev. Ball returned, he sent an invitation to them to stay at his house instead of the hotel, but with four adults and a baby, they graciously turned down his offer.

The city streets reminded George of the pictures seen in missionary books and magazines of the barelegged men or those:

> dressed in baggy white clothes and wearing turbans or little caps, the women in gay colors with rings in fingers and toes, noses and ears, and all with that peculiarly graceful carriage which comes from carrying everything they can on their heads.[4]

He wrote a glowing estimate of the British presence:

> There is no difficulty in discovering who are the rulers of India. Everywhere Englishmen are giving the orders and the natives are executing them.... England has done wonders for India, has given good roads, public wells, schools, protection, has abolished many forms of oppression, built railroads, and now is trying to put their cities in proper sanitary condition. When you see India, you realize that the English have a genius for government.[5]

George and Samuel visited a Rev. Mr. Waller who led the American Methodist Mission of the Eurasians and Europeans.[6] He and his family resided in a nicely furnished home with pictures, art, and a piano like a house in the United States. The noticeable difference to George was that his own friends were missing from the house. He did not think the Wallers' living conditions were a great hardship compared to the living quarters he anticipated in Bahrain:

> Our quarters will be a native house, leaky in rainy weather and close[d] in hot weather, but 'sufficient unto the day is the evil thereof,' and you won't hear me kicking.[7]

George visited a tailor to be measured for three white suits that cost $1.25 each. When completed, the suits were shipped to Bahrain. He also bought an iron cot, mattress, and other items.[8] After dinner and prayers in the evening, he walked around the hotel compound to enjoy some alone time and reflect on the day. Looking up, he saw a moon so bright it outshone any he had seen in New York because of the latitude.

George devoted five hours to his Arabic studies on Thursday. He translated simple sentences from a vocabulary of about seventy-five words as Samuel spoke them to him. A month earlier, he only knew the Arabic alphabet. Samuel was a good teacher because he made Arabic clear.

The Rev. Frederick Barny arrived from Busrah, Iraq on Friday, September 30. He had joined the Arabian Mission in 1897 and had been learning Arabic in Busrah. He was Margaret's fiancé. He used a lot of time upon arrival in Karachi to locate a minister to officiate at his and Margaret's wedding ceremony the next day.[9] The British garrison chaplain, Rev. A. B. Howard, agreed to officiate.

Saturday morning, the wedding party met Rev. Howard at his house where the proper declarations were sworn. Then they all traveled to Holy Trinity Cathedral where the wedding was conducted.[10] Samuel gave Margaret away, George stood up for Frederick, and Amy and Katarina were sympathizing friends. Frederick and Margaret became husband and wife. Frederick arranged a breakfast at the Reynolds

Hotel in town for the reception. The Barnys sailed to Muscat, Oman a week later.

What George saw and heard concerning the Christian presence in India, he shared with his parents:

> The missions are doing something for these people but, as everywhere in India, the people are so many and the Christian workers so few. Yet when the results are compared with the results from the same expenditure of money and effort at home, it is evident that the Lord has especially favored the work of foreign missions.[11]

George and the Zwemers departed Karachi on the *Kola* for the last leg of their journey. They made a stop in Bunder Abbar, Persia, or Bandar Abbas, Iran, today, where he bought a Persian rug.[12]

PART III

BAHRAIN

CHAPTER 12

On the Mission Field

"At last—Bahrain! It has taken us a long time to get here, but I hope now that moving days are over."[1] These words of relief from two months of sailing were all that George wrote on Friday, October 14 because he arrived at Bahrain with a fever. He came down ill while on the steamer from Karachi.[2] He quoted a friend's cliché, "'I didn't care whether school kept or not,'" meaning he did not have much gumption about anything.[3]

George and the Zwemers went ashore at Manama, located on the northern shore of Bahrain Island. They were quarantined because of the fever near an old Portuguese fort about three miles west of town.[4] They left most of their luggage on the boat. They spent the first night under a hut made of date boughs and an old sail laid on top of the boughs. The next day, their servant Davoud (David) brought a small tent for George to use. The Zwemers cared for him under these primitive conditions with limited amounts of food. George thought they were living like caged zoo animals, where everyone could gaze at them, but they could not leave.

Bahrain is a nation of one large island and many small ones in the southwestern portion of the Persian Gulf about fifteen miles off the southeastern coast of Saudi Arabia. The Gulf of Bahrain separates the islands from Arabia. The name means "two seas." Al Muharraq was the nineteenth-century capital located on Muharraq Island, a short distance from Manama on the northeast portion of the largest and main island. The nation of islands' population was about 50,000 in 1898. Due to its world-famous pearls, it has been called the "Pearl Island."

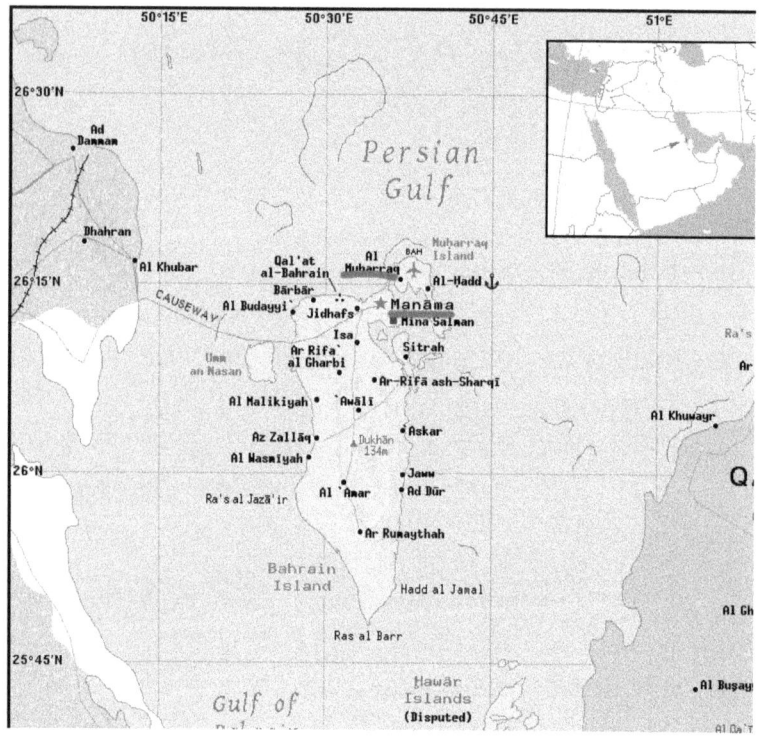

Bahrain: Manama and Al Muharraq underlined[5]

The appearance and economic status of modern Bahrain is in sharp contrast to the rustic and poor conditions George encountered. The discovery of oil in the early twentieth century fueled its astonishing transformation. Its history stretches back to at least 2500 BCE. The ruins of a fifteenth-century Portuguese fort are located on the site of many ancient archaeological remains. The British presence in Bahrain gained prominence in the nineteenth century. Through various treaties with the ruling family, the British assumed the defense of the island. The ruling family agreed to refrain from war, piracy, and slavery.[6]

Bahrain is hot and dry during most of the year. Rainfall is minimal, about three inches a year. The average daily temperature rises from 90° Fahrenheit in mid-April to 100° from June to September, and then decreases to 90°. Temperatures are lower from November to March. Humidity is between 72 and 80 percent.[7]

George and the Zwemers returned to the boat to retrieve the rest of their belongings when they were released from quarantine. The task was harder than they imagined, and somewhat humorous. The boat was anchored about a mile offshore due to the shallow water from the low tide. They attempted to ride donkeys to the boat and to carry the luggage to shore. Donkeys can be stubborn creatures, and so it was with the ones Samuel, Amy, and George rode on. George ended up being carried by a man out to the boat. It took five men to coax the donkey Amy rode. Once everything arrived on shore, they visited the Bahraini British agent Mohamed Rahum, who gave them permission to move into the Mission house.[8]

The Mission house was like the surrounding houses. The two stories were built around a courtyard. It was so close to the sea that high tide flowed in and out of the first floor. One door on the other side of the house opened to the street. The dining room windows overlooked the sea and provided a beautiful view while eating meals. The room also served as a general-purpose area with an organ and chairs. A large vacant room remained empty for some reason. A third first-floor front room served as the dispensary for patients where, "Mr. Zwemer performs wonderful cures of fever, ulcers, etc., but does not pretend to be a 'bakeena' or doctor."[9]

The house was also used to receive women who came to visit Amy. The separation of genders was important in the Muslim culture. Christian literature and Bibles were sold at the house. Eventually, a shop in the market was rented for selling the literature.

Nothing was straight about the house construction. The three rooms on the second floor were on three different levels. One served as the Zwemers' bedroom. The study at the north end of the house became George's bedroom and a receiving room for callers. This dual purpose meant that unscheduled visitors interrupted his language studies. He believed the large vacant room on the ground floor could be used for receiving visitors to eliminate many of the distractions.

Rev. Zwemer had served in Bahrain several times between December 1892[10] and 1896.[11] He and Amy served there together during the last quarter of 1896 following their wedding. They had not painted a rosy picture of the island for George. He anticipated his parents' question:

> I suppose you are curious to know what I think of Bahrain now that I have seen it and whether it equals my expectations. Well, I think it does and considering I had no expectations, they could not very well be disappointed. The Zwemers never boasted about the place except as a good opportunity for work, and on the steamer all the officers regarded it as the jumping off place. So, I had no chance for beautiful pictures of the imagination.[12]

He expected Bahrain to be his home for at least a year. He began his immersion in Arab culture on this Persian Gulf island.

Samuel recruited three Bahraini servants to assist with the household chores. Davoud, or David, was the leader. Samuel had found him homeless on a street after he was evicted from his stepmother's house. He became the cook and served as the jack of all trades. Mahommed [sic] was a small Persian lad who swept the floors, sprinkled water on the courtyard to keep the dust down, and ran errands. He did not speak Arabic, but Davoud understood his language. The third servant, Ali, waited tables and took care of the bedrooms, if George kept at him. George followed these brief descriptions of the servants by stating:

Verily the Orient is a strange land and Arabs are not Yankees in gumption, but they are not such a bad lot, and they get things done after a while, but you always have to allow for lost motion. And so, we are living together, Christians and [Muslims], and so it is the world over except in Turkey. God hasten the time when they will serve the Lord Jesus and the stagnation of Islam be taken from their lives.[13]

CHAPTER 13

Arabic, Arabic, Arabic

George and the Zwemers continued to get settled in the Mission house. Their small worshiping congregation held their morning services in the general-purpose room. Being in a religious minority as a Christian, George reported homesickness for his larger hometown congregation:

> where the church bells ring and several hundred people assemble every week to honor the Lord our God. Here there is no Sabbath.[1] Only in our own house is the day honored, for all about us [is] nothing but [Islam]. We have been keeping it as best we can, but the contrast makes me homesick for Christian fellowship and a chance to join in the songs of Zion and to hear Mr. Bayless pray and preach. We have sung and prayed together and studied the Bible and read papers and magazines a month or two old and enjoyed them none the less because of their antiquity.[2]

George wished he could celebrate Thanksgiving with his parents, but since he could not, maybe his brothers would visit them, or his parents would pick up their son Harry at Auburn Seminary to visit their other two sons' families in Dolgeville, New York. He eagerly awaited copies of the Mexico *Independent* and *The Evangelist* magazine. He had devoured the months-old August and September editions of the *Cosmopolitan*.

George's waiting didn't last long. Mail arrived at the house during their Sunday morning worship.[3] They paused their service to examine the mail. George's stack of mail included four letters, copies of *The Evangelist* up to September 8, and October's *Scribner's Magazine*. He read his pastor's brief article on the farewell service for him in August's *The Evangelist*.[4]

George laid out to his parents his daily schedule:

6:30 a.m.	Arise
7:00 -11:30	Breakfast; Prayers
	Read Genesis in Arabic with Samuel
	Study Arabic on his own
11:30 -1:00	Lunch; prayer; meditation on a Missionary Psalm, most likely Psalm 96
	Arabic on his own
1:00 – 2:00	Arabic with Bahraini teacher Subakh
	Arabic on his own
3:00 – 5:00	Tea
	Arabic on his own
5:00 – 6:30	Walk or work around the house
6:30	Dinner
	Read Arabic with Samuel. Gospel of John translation; focus on grammar.
	Organize the day's work; write letters.

George devoted most of his day to various types of Arabic studies. He had two teachers, Rev. Zwemer and the native teacher Subakh, and also studied on his own. The work included reading Genesis, translating John's Gospel, and reading other Arabic texts. George found Arabic difficult to pronounce correctly. The gutturals were throat scrapers that challenge beginners. The word construction is different from English. Each word has a root to which are added prefixes, suffixes, and infixes, which go between the prefixes and suffixes. Like other languages, Arabic has its dialects with their own unique features.[5] Some people call Arabic the "language of angels" for how beautiful it sounds, but it is still a hard language to learn and master.

Davoud prepared the meals. Breakfast consisted of rolled oats, eggs, and bread. A local baker made a European form of bread that was more to their liking than the flat, thin native bread called Khubez. Lunch might be fish, mutton, potatoes, eggplant, and bread. The supper's menu was like the noon meal—potatoes, eggplant, marrow, mutton, pudding, and bread and jam. Davoud prepared first-rate meals.

George boasted about the famous dates grown in Arabia and Bahrain. Fresh ones excelled the ones shipped to the United States. Periodically, uninvited guests such as lizards and water rats appeared in the house looking for the dates or other scraps of food, but they were not harmful.

George's three white suits arrived from Karachi. They fit exactly right, were collarless, and buttoned at the throat. Neckties were unnecessary. The three suits and delivery cost $4.50.[6] After donning one of the suits, he told his parents:

> If you saw me coming along with [hat], white clothes and full beard, the latter a thing of beauty and joy forever, you might be at a loss to tell where you had seen me before.[7]

He had grown a handsome beard since leaving home.

Another trunk arrived in good shape, and the contents survived except for the glass of two unidentified framed photos. Glass became a commodity on the island after the Mission station was founded, so replacing the broken panes was not a problem. Other luggage had yet to arrive. George bought some boards and additional tools to supplement those Samuel owned. He planned to build a table for his study.

Two young men visited the mission Wednesday night, November 2, and said ten of them were reading a gospel together. They wanted a copy of the five books of Moses, but only a one-volume copy of

Genesis and Matthew was available. George surmised, "There may be other such groups. So far they are only curious and interested. May the reading bring conviction."[8]

George asked his parents how his Aunt Lydia was doing and if she had yet reconciled herself to him becoming an Arab.[9] He also expressed appreciation for Arthur Becker, a businessman in Mexico who attended the Presbyterian Church. George had shared some rewarding conversations with Becker that summer that had encouraged him. He wished his parents a Merry Christmas and Happy New Year because his next letter would arrive after the holidays.

He attributed the safe journey to Bahrain to all his church's prayers:

> You wrote of how frequently I am prayed for, I felt sure it would be so, but I am glad to know that so many earnest petitions ascend to God for me. When I think of our long voyage practically without a hitch, of our freedom from anything like serious illness, of the ease with which I have been able to take up hard study after so long a vacation, and the attitude of the people here, so free from hostility in the main, I feel that prayer has already been answered and will be in the future.[10]

Samuel received the extremely sad news that his younger brother, the Rev. Peter Zwemer, had died at the Presbyterian Hospital in New York City on October 18. His sickness had puzzled the doctors. The Arabian Mission had lost a great asset. He had given his life to Arabia; now, who would take his place? Peter's death added fuel to the call for more recruits.

The Bahrain station received an additional staff person with the arrival of a thirty-year-old Syrian Arab colporteur, book and literature seller, named Elias. He was associated with the American Board of Missions north of Baghdad in Iraq. He had joined the church six years earlier. He spoke Arabic and Turkish, but no English. George thought his

Arabic was better than that of the natives of Bahrain. Elias demonstrated earnestness and skill. Since George's Arabic teacher, Subakh, was sick, Elias substituted as his language teacher. They started with the first few verses of John's Gospel and sang Arabic songs.

An Arab who had made trouble at the Bible shop the week before came to the house with a little boy and they showed great interest in the organ and the Arabic hymns: "'Ahjeeb, ahjeeb!' 'wonderful, wonderful,' they said." After they left, Samuel and Elias went on an outreach to a little village nearby. There, they had a good time talking to the people and sold two Gospels. They found a man in a hut who possessed a Persian Gospel that he had bought two years earlier. It was all thumbed through and written over, showing it had been used a lot. The man still prized it and kept it wrapped in a cloth in a box to keep it out of his neighbors' sight.

In the evening, an intelligent-looking man from the mainland region of Katif visited the house.[11] He had heard Mr. Zwemer preach in the marketplace and came to get a New Testament. He was going back to the mainland in three or four weeks. They thought he might open the way for Elias to visit the mainland. George made it clear about these personal contacts:

> These are little instances, yet they show how the leaven is at work. There is a widespread feeling amongst [Muslims] that their glory has departed, and they begin to seek the better way. It is slowly moving now. The momentum will come later.[12]

The trouble at the Bible shop mentioned above was witnessed by George. It arose when Samuel preached in the shop. He preached "plainly," by which he meant boldly or forthrightly. Samuel told his Muslim audience that the Quran was not the book of God and Muhammad was not a prophet of God. Some of the men were deeply offended by these remarks and reacted angrily. After they heard him state such blasphemous things, they declared, "'Astaghfer Allah!' i.e., 'I ask forgiveness of God.'" Samuel then took a copy of the Quran to prove a point, but the men snatched it out of his hands and ran off with it. They thought he was too unclean to touch their holy book. The men went to some of the sheikhs to report what they had heard Samuel say about the Quran and Muhammad.

The next morning, a man was stationed opposite the shop to warn everyone to keep away from the Bible shop by order of the main sheikh. Samuel took advantage of this situation by reading the Gospel to the watchman and talking to him while Elias went out into the market and sold more books than he had at the shop on previous days. George's later assessment stated:

> We think that the disturbance has done more good than harm, and as so often has happened, 'God makes the wrath of man to praise him and the remainder of wrath he will restrain.' [see Psalm 76:10].[13]

Samuel disagreed with many aspects of Islam's creed, theology, and practices. Even so, he cared about the souls of Arabs because the purpose of Jesus Christ's death included them. He loved Arabs daily in the clinic, on the streets, and in the market, but how did his plain preaching concur with his teaching in his presentation "Personal Dealing, The Great Missionary Method" at the February Student Volunteer Movement Convention in Cleveland? In the presentation, he stressed that most missionaries would speak to small groups of people or individuals, not to hundreds or thousands of native people. Personal dealings with native people required faith, love, and patience. Samuel told his convention audience that he wrote the word "Arabs" in his Bible at 1 Corinthians 13, the love chapter. He read the chapter with the word Arabs in the verses to drive home his point that one must love others for missionary efforts to be of value.[14] Samuel gave George a lot to think about in proclaiming plainly his opinions about Islam's creed and serving Arabs with faith, love, and patience.

George visited his Arabic teacher, Subakh, one Sunday afternoon. He had failed to show up at the house to teach Arabic during the previous week. Subakh was sick in bed in his little room, just big enough for a bed and one or two people to sit beside him. He said he was getting better and he would be at the house on Wednesday to teach, "'Inshallah,' 'If God wills.'" Subakh did not show up, so George planned to visit him again.

George thought about Thanksgiving Day in the United States in late November.[15] He imagined the weather being colder in his hometown than in Bahrain; however, a heavy rain fell two days before and a stiff wind blew. He and the Zwemers feasted on a Thanksgiving meal in the evening, which was a very good one, even without pumpkin pie. He shared sentimental reflections on the holiday:

> About New Year's I shall hear how you spent Thanksgiving and I hope you were not alone. The day is a family festival and then, if ever, they ought to be together. When these days of rejoicing come around they remind us of the homeland as nothing else does and makes us wish that we might by some enchantment be transported to America for the day and be back again to our work the next.[16]

He switched to the topic work, maybe to lessen his sadness while thinking about the family so far away:

> There is a wonderful attractiveness about this work when you feel that, in God's providence, the responsibility all rests upon yourself, and if you do not speak then no one will hear.[17]

His calling as an evangelist and to serve in Arabia motivated him in his Arabic studies. He needed a strong compulsion to study Arabic to pass his Arabic examination at the end of his first year:

This has been the great incentive to me in studying Arabic, which otherwise would become a great bore, so that I have made good progress. I sent you a copy of the gospel of John in Arabic a few weeks ago and hope it has reached you. I have already read it through at sight and seven chapters carefully and will soon finish it. To pass my first year's examinations I must know all four gospels and some Arabic books besides, also must be able to change English to Arabic and to converse with an Arab.[18]

Rev. Zwemer decided that Elias should replace Subakh as George's Arabic teacher. Subakh was not dependable. Elias and George taught each other. Elias learned English from George in the evenings, and Elias taught him Arabic during the day. George thought he got more Arabic out of Elias than Elias got English from him.

A Banian merchant-boy visited the Mission house to inquire about Christianity.[19] He had stopped believing in Hinduism and wondered if the white people might have the true faith. He appeared sincere to George, was straightforward, and sounded like a good candidate to find the light.

The next morning, the postmaster and his wife, both Goanese, paid a visit that ruined George's study time. Their long visit irritated him. Such visitors didn't know when to leave.

Three other incidences gave George and the Zwemers the impression that they had some good friends in Bahrain. The Wednesday before Thanksgiving, a highly intelligent Muslim arrived at the house. He did not describe himself as a good Muslim because he held to some of the things Islam taught but rejected other ones. He wrote a letter on behalf of the Arabian Mission to the British agent in Bushire, Persia, to report that people were interfering with the Bible shop selling good books. The letter pertained to the watchman who was posted across the street from the Bible shop to warn people not to buy books in the shop. The second incident was remarkably similar to the first one. Another man wrote a letter to the British agent about the commotion at the Bible shop. A Banian man, different than the one mentioned above, told Samuel that he and his friends were praying that he would not leave the island because he was so successful in healing fevers. George summarized, "The disturbance at the Bible shop has really helped us and sales have increased if anything."[20]

Elias took George on a tour of Al-Muharraq on the island by the same name. They waded ashore about a half mile because of low tide. They were tempted to turn back because of the low tide and because they knew the mail had arrived in Manama. People bought seven gospels in the market in comparison to none sold the previous week when Samuel and Elias visited the town. George and Elias were happy they had pushed ahead and completed the outreach. Both men looked forward to reading their mail.

To dispel misconceptions back home, George humorously reported that he did not live in a tent surrounded by camels and Arabian horses.[21] Manama was a town of 5,000 people. There were very few camels or horses. Donkeys were the prevalent beast of burden. They were strong animals and could carry a person at a good speed, especially if a boy ran behind the donkey and regularly applied the persuader, or prod. Unfortunately for the animals, many boys were cruel and their goading kept the wounds festering on the donkeys. Davoud connected the treatment of the donkey to Psalm 74:20, "the dark places of the earth are full of the habitations of cruelty."[22]

The few horses in Manama were ordinary ones. A man tried to sell a gray one to George that was three-and-a-half years old for $100 in US currency. He thought it was worth about $50. The cattle on the island provided milk, butter, and some meat occasionally, but they were not in his area. The natives also raised black sheep and goats. Their hens laid eggs not much bigger than bantam eggs, which range from one to two ounces each. Chickens were scrawny with very little meat on the bones. They were adapted to the country's climate. George's father's Plymouth Rock chickens would probably sweat to death if they were raised in Bahrain. He thought he would get a better understanding of the domesticated animals when he toured more of the island.

The Arabs were uniformly sparsely built and he had seen only one fat man. They were also straight and wiry. Some of the sheikhs (the town leaders) wore flowing robes and bright turbans or bead cloths that were very attractive. Their attire added dignity. Seriousness was characteristic of the people and the boisterous mirth of Americans was conspicuously absent. George saw little boys ten to twelve years old dressed just like men and carrying canes like old men. In contrast to the Arabs, the African population on the island was happy-go-lucky and carefree. Poor people were scantily clothed with non-colorful, dirty cotton garments.

Muslim women of all classes, except the lowest of the low, covered their faces with an opening for only one eye. They glided through the streets like outcasts. No one was supposed to look at them. They were too far beneath the men to deserve the men's notice. Their condition was a definite proof of the evil nature of Islam. It could not be from God.

The people as a whole were outwardly deeply religious. Mosques were located all around Manama. Five times a day a muezzin, the one who called Muslims to prayer, sang from each mosque.[23] The calls to prayer were simply part of the outward formality of Islam but, beneath the formality, the religion was as bad as one could imagine. George's assessments confirmed to him what Samuel had gleaned from conversations with Arab leaders.

George thought Arabs had sinned so long under the sanction of Islam that the sense of sin was almost gone, and their consciences were seared. The description in Philippians 3:18-19, "enemies of the cross," fit them precisely,[24] though the Muslims he had met possessed many good qualities. Their seared consciences did not appear on the surface, but the attitude of their hearts toward God was awful. They were full of the fruit of the old Pharisees. They had a form of godliness, but they denied the power of it.[25] Accordingly, George knew there was not another people group in the world who needed the good news more than the Arabs.

The two privations George experienced in Bahrain were friends and Christian privileges, which probably referred to the "Christianized" culture at home. In spite of this, George was glad God sent him to Bahrain:

> I don't think anyone thought more of their friends than I, and God knows I would never have left them for anything else but His work. I have no regrets, however, and am glad that God called me and would not let me go until I consented. I am only impatient to get at the work itself and get out of constant study of Arabic.[26]

CHAPTER 14

The Awkward Squad

George found his spirit caught between language training and outreach. Learning Arabic would help him communicate effectively with the people of Bahrain. However, his eagerness to engage in missionary work made his language studies feel like a bother at times. Fortunately, his taste of serving in the Bible shop, touring, and welcoming strangers to the Mission house reminded him that his time would come in due season.

Samuel and George walked to an old, ruined mosque on Thursday, December 1, about two or three miles away, where a market was held every Thursday.[1] Several hundred Arabs were selling their wares or purchasing items. The ancient mosque's roof had caved in, the walls were crumbled, and only two minarets, seventy-five or one hundred feet tall, remained standing. They climbed one of them and enjoyed the magnificent view of the Persian Gulf to the west, north, and east. Turning south, they saw about two-thirds of the length of the island. The portion closest to them was green with date orchards and fields of clover for the donkeys. Irrigation from fountains and springs watered the orchards and fields.

The missionaries devoted most of their time examining the Cufic,[2] a calligraphy script, and Arabic inscriptions, and climbing the minaret. Consequently, Samuel did not have time to preach in the market, but he did talk to a small group of men. They said there had been talk of rebuilding the mosque, but the community leaders kept the money for themselves and the repairs were never made. The men admitted the glory of Islam had departed from the area. Though in ruins, the mosque left enough evidence of a once-glorious era in Bahrain that far exceeded what the two visitors saw.

George drew a map of the island for his parents with short descriptions of the main points of interest. He did not think Europeans had thoroughly explored the southern part of the island. He and Samuel considered that portion of the island as a future objective for outreach. Ideas for such ministry percolated in George's mind later:

> We ought to be at these markets every week with books and preaching, as well as on constant tours to the villages on this and adjacent islands.... There is a world of work to be done on these islands, to say nothing of the mainland.[3]

But the time was not right for it:

> We can't do it yet. If we get a teacher from Busrah [Iraq] next month he can tend the Bible shop besides teaching me, and Elias can go on the road.[4]

Speaking of the Bible shop, George tended it twice on his own. He was elated that he had begun to help some, even though lacking fluency with Arabic hindered his usefulness. He used his listening skills to increase his comprehension of the language.

Extra mail arrived from Mumbai (Bombay) on Friday, December 2. Letters, papers, and the first copy of the *Times of India* arrived. The *Times* brought the Mission house up to date to November 26 on international news, which was better than getting five-week-old news from America. Speaking of mail, George thought it would be better to use a mimeograph machine to decrease the amount of time he spent writing to so many people. He figured his parents could calculate when his letters would arrive to soften their loneliness:

I don't wonder that you are [lonesome] though, but God is very near. I am sorry I wrote anything about the fever for it did not last long and I am afraid you have been anxious in consequence. I never felt better than I do now.[5]

Three steamers graced the harbor the first week of December. This was an unusual occurrence at Manama. Two steamers arrived from Mumbai (Bombay), India, and one from Busrah, Iraq. An Arab said that so many ships in the harbor made it appear like a European harbor. One steamer carried 11,000 bags of rice and the regular mail steamer brought 3,000 more. The two shipments filled the customhouse enclosure, but the bags did not stay long. A large amount of the rice stayed on the island, and the balance went to the mainland.

What really excited George and the Zwemers even more about the steamers' arrival was the additional boxes that arrived from New York. George's boxes contained his college and seminary books. He sarcastically remarked that he had not missed them because of his constant use of Palmer's Arabic grammar and the Arabic gospels.[6] His plan to work on Arabic on Saturday might take second place to unpacking the boxes. Time management issues reminded him of the importance of his studies so he would not have to repeat them. Dr. Guilan Lansing, a former Presbyterian missionary to Syria and Egypt, once declared:

> I would rather traverse Africa from Alexandria to the Cape of Good Hope than to attempt a second time to master the Arabic language.[7]

George added his own motivational commentary to keep his priorities straight:

> No slipshod knowledge will do. The learned Arabs have almost a reverence for the language, and for a missionary to murder the language is often to close the door to their hearts.[8]

Elias made friends with an Armenian surgeon attached to the Turkish army. He was on his way to Hosa, the chief city of the province by the same name on the Arabian mainland.[9] A trip with the doctor might open a great opportunity for Elias to travel to Arabia to sell books. He was eager to go, but a departure date was difficult to arrange because of the laziness of the local sailors. When the wind was fair, it took them too long to get ready; when the wind was too strong, they waited for it to calm down. As a result, eager travelers had to be patient. George criticized this habit of the natives folding their arms and putting all the responsibility on God by saying, "It is God's will," until better conditions arrived. This attitude served to hinder all activity and forethought, even in everyday matters.

George assumed the Arabs were impressed with the superior civilization of the western Christian nations, including their wealth, material comforts, learning, science, and inventions. However, they explained it all away by declaring that Allah gave the Christian nations the great blessings now and withheld the blessings from the Muslims—true believers—until the hereafter. The tables would be turned on the Christian nations. Muslims would then glory in their sensual paradise while they exulted over the tortures of the infidels in the flames of hell. George thought it was a wonderfully comfortable way of shutting their eyes to what Christianity had done for the world. Their attitude was pitiful, but George had to learn to tolerate it.

He unpacked and arranged the contents of his boxes. Nothing of consequence was damaged in his belongings. His beautiful little organ was in splendid shape. It produced enough volume for a good-sized congregation, if they could gather one together. The walls in his room had little recesses about two feet by four feet and one foot deep. He used them for storing the cases and extra books. Seeing all the books on the shelves renewed his love for them. His Arabic studies made him think he would not care for the books, but his delight in them quickly returned. George had felt cut off from educated and thinking people, but the books connected him to them again. He would enjoy reading them during the winter.

George and Samuel's combined book collections made a splendid library. Samuel's books on Arabia and Islam were about as fine a collection as could be found almost anywhere. George thought those in French and German were the best.

Flies became a problem in the house. They were so thick that George and the Zwemers ate their meals like the Jews who had rebuilt the walls of Jerusalem during the days of Nehemiah—a weapon in one hand and working with the other hand.[10] George and Samuel made a screen door for the dining room with the netting that came with the luggage. It eliminated the flies in the house and meals were eaten in peace once again.

Speaking of peace, President William McKinley signed The Treaty of Peace, or Treaty of Paris, in Paris, France, on December 10. The treaty officially ended the Spanish-American War, and by it, the United States acquired the Philippines, Puerto Rico, and Guam. Spain also gave up all claim of sovereignty over and title to Cuba.[11]

Captain Brander visited the Mission house and stayed overnight. The British government in India sent him to Manama to inspect some arms stored in the city. Arms shipments were going to Arabia, Persia, and Afghanistan through Bahrain. The British tried to stop or control illegal arms shipments.[12]

Around the middle of December, George sent a reply to Dr. M. Woolsey Stryker, president of Hamilton College, who had inquired about the Arabic studies.[13] He had learned the main principles of grammar, was ready to study them in more depth, carefully translated eight chapters in John's gospel, and read the whole gospel by sight plus chapters in the other gospels. His teacher corrected his pronunciation less frequently, and he was making himself understood in simple conversations. George estimated he knew three hundred Arabic words for conversations and reading. He calculated that by the New Year, he would finish the Gospel of John, and perhaps Mark's Gospel. His goals were to sit in the Bible shop and converse with people, read the whole New Testament by the end of his first year of language study, preach a sermon in Arabic, and engage in intelligent conversations. If he could crack the backbone of grammar and translation, the rest of his improvement would come by use as with all languages.

George told President Stryker that the Arabic Bible was probably the best translation ever made. A critic boasted that the only trouble with the Arabic Bible was that it surpassed the Hebrew, Aramaic, and Greek the Bible books were originally written in, and he received new light on the Bible by studying it in Arabic. Studying different languages can have this effect on people's understanding.

He asked President Stryker to pray for the Holy Spirit's work in the Arabs' lives. Argument and exhortation were in vain with them if the Spirit did not open their hearts to receive the truth. He looked forward to when he would use Arabic to strike a blow to break the shackles from the people's darkened hearts.

On Christmas Day, George could not get it through his head that it was Christmas because the weather was so different there compared to in New York. Pick any particularly bright, pleasant day in October in New York and call it Christmas to get an idea of what the weather was like in Bahrain. He and the Zwemers did not celebrate the holiday to any great extent. The postmaster and two Goanese friends, all Catholics, joined them in the morning for their little worship service in the mejlis or meeting room.[14] Mrs. Zwemer served a delicious Christmas dinner at noon, and George made sure he did his part that none of it went to waste.

George wrote a good report to Mr. Humphries, the editor of the Mexico *Independent,* about the newspaper's reception in the Mission house:

We get quite interested in the foreign correspondence of the MEXICO INDEPENDENT out here. Mr. and Mrs. Zwemer like to read them and laugh over some of the experiences which they call to mind.[15]

George appreciated Mr. Humphries' support of his mission work by printing excerpts from his letters.

The daily routine of Arabic studies did not provide much variation from day to day. One Arab amused him on Christmas Day by telling him that if Muhammad had not been buried in the earth, it would be shaking continually. The man also said that the Patriarch Joseph, Jacob's son, invented the watch when he was in prison, giving George the impression that Arabs thought they knew everything.[16] The man saw the several hundred books on the shelves and looked through the great *Funk & Wagnalls Standard Dictionary*. Maybe he left with a glimmering suspicion that the Americans might know something, even if they had not heard that Joseph invented the watch.

George and Samuel could not let the legends alone, so they asked a learned man in Manama about Joseph's invention. He replied that the other man was ignorant and knew nothing about it. Joseph had not invented the watch, but Enoch had. Enoch had been taken up to the fourth heaven where he saw how the sun, moon, and stars moved. From these observations, he received the idea to make a watch. George presumed that next he would hear that Methuselah invented watches to keep track of his age. Though he viewed the stories as nonsense, he put a positive spin on them:

> You see by this we can learn something every day in Bahrain. If the learned people believe such yarns you will not wonder that the poor people are firm believers in Djinus[17]—genii—and the evil eye.[18]

The biography of James Gilmore also occupied him on Christmas Day.[19] Gilmore was a Scottish missionary to Mongolia from 1870 to 1891. George described him as a true hero of the cross of Christ whose devotion equaled that of the apostle Paul himself. He easily saw the correlation of Gilmore's work to his work with Arabs:

> It will require just such men to open up the interior of Arabia one of these days. Just when it can be done it is hard to say.[20]

Gilmore's story inspired George with his devotion to learn the Chinese and Mongol languages, make efforts to reach the Mongolian nomads and Chinese with the good news of Jesus, and embrace their cultures. He saw few converts from his labors, and this turned out to be the same for the Arabian Mission.

George awaited word about Elias' trip to Hosa on the Arabian mainland. A month had passed, and he wondered what kind of attitudes Elias had found among the people and government toward the Mission's attempt at presenting the good news in that city and province.

Captain Brander, mentioned above, earned a few more remarks because the natives' lengthy delays and lies broke the captain's patience.[21] He thought Manama was an awful place and threatened to send a damning report about it to the British Government. George concurred that no one in their right mind would pick Bahrain to do business, seek health, or for any of the other reasons for choosing a place to live.

The Arabian Mission's aim of propagating the good news of Jesus Christ, however, tempered George's reactions to the natives. He and the Zwemers did not find the natives as distasteful as the captain did. Like the captain, George found it hard not to despise the people who were liars and hypocrites, but he was in Manama to point such people to Christ. He drew from his own experience to illustrate that the Arabs were liars and hypocrites. A young man came into the Bible shop one day. He swore by God, by the prophet Muhammad, by his beard, and everything he could think of as he told George that he would return in ten minutes to buy a book. He never returned. This example sounds petty, but the man's religious oaths put his words in a more serious category in George's mind. He had seen enough of the natives' broken promises to make him sick of them. He concluded this story by stating:

> It is a perpetual marvel to them that we speak the truth. That man in Liverpool who called Americans the greatest liars evidently never visited Bahrain.[22]

George started teaching English to a nine-year-old boy named Abdul Kareem. Abdul was accompanied by a servant about the same age. This allowed George to make friends and learn Arabic. He remembered Paul's metaphor in his letter to the Galatians that the Jewish law was the "pedagogos" or servant that brings us to Christ. George was the schoolmaster, and the servant boy was the pedagogos bringing Abdul to him for his English instruction. Abdul made worthwhile progress in learning the Yankee dialect while George learned Arabic from the two boys. Teaching English served as another form of being an actual missionary. He did not aspire to be an English teacher, but education was highly respected in Muslim lands.

He gave another critical assessment of Islam with an erroneous conclusion:

> Islam cannot bear the light. If ever it shall come to pass that education shall become the rule and not the exception in [Muslim] lands they will have long since ceased to be [Muslims]. Their faith rests on such an amount of error and contradictions that they dare not investigate Christianity unless they find themselves unable [any] longer to hold their old beliefs and practice their old sins.[23]

He believed that the intellectual and moral content of Christianity was superior to Islam. Muslims would embrace Christianity if they received a thorough explanation of it.

Rev. Zwemer's plain speaking style continued to occupy George's mind. Zwemer:

> speaks to them with great boldness and plainness of speech and they have long since discovered that they are no match for him.[24]

Boldness and plainness of speech are commendable communication skills, but if they are used to simply win arguments, they miss the mark for a Christian evangelist. George thought Samuel was winning the arguments with his audiences. Samuel forthrightly rejected elements of Islam's creed and declared the good news, but he knew that true faith comes from a person's heart and not solely by intellectual assent.[25]

George prepared to conclude his Christmas Day letter by stating:

> The Lord has wonderfully blessed me, and I only hope that I may be given grace to do faithfully the drudgery of this first year—incessant language study. The temptation to get lazy and to shirk is almost unconquerable at times.[26]

He and the Zwemers awaited word about the annual Mission meeting to be held in Busrah. Turkish authorities were interfering with the dispensary there, which made them anxious to hear how the conditions there stood. He added that Frederick and Margaret Barny, the newlyweds, were in Muscat having quite a time repairing the house they lived in. One wall of the house fell, causing great discomfort. He thought Mrs. Barny viewed it as his Uncle Amos used to call such situations a "boss experience."[27]

George spent more time in the Bible shop learning additional things about the local culture. Customers took advantage of his ignorance of

Arabic and money. They paid for literature with coins that were not acceptable elsewhere. He put a spin on this embarrassing situation by stating that it was increasing his collection of curious coins, even if they were not valuable. An African gave him an east African coin to buy a gospel instead of a coin from India.[28] Another man offered him half price for a gospel. The man said something to him about drinking and at the same time made motions of cutting up the gospel. It came to George later that night that Arabs called smoking cigarettes "drinking tobacco." The man tried to make him understand that the paper the gospel was printed on would be good for rolling cigarettes.

About a dozen Muslims visited the Mission house the afternoon after Christmas. George did not explain the reason for the visit or what they talked about. He said they seemed to enjoy the time. One night, a young Banian merchant from India stopped at the house for medicine. He asked if an eclipse would occur that night.[29] According to his Hindu religion, an eclipse was caused by a demon swallowing the moon. It was the best time to wash clothes, but he did not say why.[30] George did not think it was a good time to wash clothes because the temperature had been 55 degrees Fahrenheit or lower all day. He was pleased the Bible did not require him to wash laundry on such a cold night. A strong cold north[31] wind blew that week, forcing them to bundle up in their overcoats and shawls even in the house.

George served in the Bible shop again during the morning and afternoon. He engaged a young lad from India, who was reading the New Testament in English. The boy seemed like a sincere inquirer. George rejoiced in having a long conversation with him and doing something in the way of missionary work, even if he could not preach in Arabic.

On the last day of 1898, George reviewed the year:

> This is the last letter to you for '98. 1899 will soon begin and I wonder if it will bring as novel experiences as has 1898. A year ago, I was carefully considering the question whether I

ought to apply to the Dutch Reformed [Mission] Board. Now the preliminaries are over, and I am a missionary in fact. I can hardly realize it myself and this past year with all its busy preparation and constant journeying seems like a dream, a dream, however, in which, as I recall how one thing has followed another.[32]

Little did he know that something novel would happen in about six weeks. He continued his reflections:

I see plainly that it has been God's leading and though I have no idea what I shall be doing next year whether I will be at Busrah, Bahrain or Muscat, touring to the interior or teaching boys in the school, or what not, I never felt more willing to trust God or confidence in His guidance. I cannot hope to have always so smooth a road as this, but I am not going to borrow trouble for the future or to hunt for disagreeable features now in order to imagine myself a martyr to the cause. I feel just the opposite at present and wonder how I ever could have dreaded it so.[33]

George touched on martyrdom a few times in his letters, especially in his sightseeing on the journey to Bahrain. He knew death was a possibility, but he did not try to manufacture circumstances to die as a martyr, as he indicated in the above remarks.

Rev. Zwemer described three types of martyrdom in his biography of Raymund Lull, in the context of Lull's martyrdom in North Africa, in the twelfth century. The first type of martyrdom contains both the will of the person and some form of violent death, epitomized by the stoning of Stephen in Acts 7:54-60. A second type of martyrdom includes the will of the person, but not a violent death. This person may die in prison. Eric Liddell died in a Japanese concentration camp in China in 1945 due to a brain tumor. The third kind of martyrdom does not include the will of the deceased. The male children killed in Bethlehem following Jesus' birth fit this category of martyrdom (Matthew 2:16). They were violently killed, but their will was not involved.[34]

George's report on January 2, 1899, told of his first experiences as a missionary for the Arabian Mission quarterly publication.[35] He reported that he had begun his service with a fever at Bahrain, and having begun with the worst, he had grown stronger every day. The reluctance and dread he had experienced when he contemplated missionary service had turned to joy and was increasingly fascinating. Despite the steamer captains and all the Europeans' disdain for Bahrain that he had heard on his travels, he found three things that commended it to a missionary. First, it stood in tremendous need of the Gospel, "Religion is here a formality, immorality well-nigh universal and honesty and truth-speaking a lost art." Second, a good beginning had begun. Previous labors broke down prejudice and generated thought and curiosity in the natives. "We have a good fighting chance with the odds on our side." Third, Bahrain was strategically located in the Persian Gulf between Muscat and Busrah, Iraq. The stand for Christ taken on Bahrain would not be limited to it, but touch the Arabian mainland.

The Mission's new appointees, Dr. Sharon and Mrs. Dr. Marion Thoms, both medical doctors, arrived on a mail steamer January 3 along with a letter from George's parents. The Thoms were on their way to Busrah, Iraq. Their arrival pleased George:

> It begins to look now as if the friends of Arabia are getting in earnest. If now our friends will see to it that the reserves are ready to hold the ground gained God will not fail of his part.[36]

The Thoms expected to stay overnight, but their departure was delayed a day. While visiting, Sharon Thoms doctored a rich Banian man. This man's condition had confounded Samuel, so Dr. Thoms served him instead of the steamer's doctor. The fee was ten rupees, about three US dollars. Banians regularly paid for their medical services, unlike most people who did not pay anything. George commented, "It is too bad that we can't have a regular doctor here all the time. Maybe we will another year."[37]

The Thoms' delayed departure became a pleasant treat for George and the Zwemers. They became better acquainted with Sharon and Marion. They felt that the Thoms were a fine addition to the Mission staff. George thought Bahrain would be their future assignment, and exactly what was needed. Assuming this to be so, he believed that when that time came, he would be more useful in Muscat with James Cantine, the other cofounder of the Mission. The transfer had to wait several months until George finished his language training. His wish about a doctor in Bahrain was granted a year later. The Thoms were assigned to Bahrain in 1900.[38]

George's new Arabic teacher, Yusuf Seesoo, arrived from Mardin, Turkey.[39] He was a bright young man who attended the American Board of Commissioners for Foreign Missions school in Mardin. He was ready to enter its theological course.[40] He would be a valuable addition to the preaching and teaching staff. The two of them did not waste any time in getting to work on Arabic:

> We have been at it hammer and tongs[41] the last four days, reading, translating English into Arabic, and writing his copy all accompanied by a great amount of broken and twisted Arabic on my part, which [Yusuf] endures good naturedly and is tickled to death when amidst all the rubbish he hears a straight sentence.[42]

Yusuf assured him that in two or three months he would talk like an Arab, which George thought showed the power of his imagination.

On a humorous note, George declared:

So far I am in the 'awkward squad,' drilling every day in Arabic, said to be one of the worst results of Babel. I have received orders to 'break its backbone' this year. In-sha-Allah.[43]

Elias returned from Hosa on the Arabian mainland, a two-days' journey inland from the Persian Gulf. The Armenian Christian Army doctor, mentioned above, took him. Elias took sixty copies of gospels or books of the Bible, which he did not try to sell until he reached the city. Upon entering Hosa, he sold about twenty-five portions in the market over several days. The Turkish officials heard of this success and ordered him to give an account of his actions to them. They claimed he did not have the right to sell the Bible portions. Elias showed them his Turkish passport, that all the portions had been printed in Beirut, which was in Turkish territory, and explained that the same kind of literature was sold freely in Busrah, which, likewise, was in Turkish territory. They did not have a case against him, but they still confiscated a few samples to send to Busrah for review by officials there. They told Elias to leave, but replied that up until their interference, he had not had any fear. Now that they had created this stir, he would not leave without protection. A detail of soldiers and horsemen escorted him out of the country with the remaining unsold books. An unconfirmed rumor said a Jewish bookstore owner offered to take the books to sell, and because of this, was fined. The Armenian doctor lost a month's wages for bringing Elias to Hosa.

George and the Zwemers rejoiced over Elias' safe return because he had been gone for a month and they had worried about him. As he told them about the trip, they heard how he had outwitted the Turkish officials in their attempt to shut down his literature selling. They laughed profusely at numerous points in his account. Elias showed himself as a levelheaded young man. The twenty-five books he sold would be read more widely because the news of the disturbance spread among the Arabs.[44] He also brought home some of the famous Khalas dates and curious-looking antique coins called "towulahs" or "long bits."[45]

George and Yusuf took a few Scriptures portions to the little coastal village of Ras Ruman.[46] They sat down with a small group of men in the street making a fish net. Yusuf talked to the men as George tried to look intelligent. One man was especially attentive, and whenever he spoke of [King] David or Christ, he would say, "Upon him be peace," which is a customary Islamic declaration of respect. He requested that coffee be brought to his visitors. The coffee was extraordinarily strong and served without milk or sugar. Each cup held about a tablespoon, but they could ask for more if they wanted it.

While they were talking with the group of men, Samuel came along wheeling Katarina in the stroller. In no time, about a hundred women and children gathered around him to admire his young daughter. She was a great attraction by herself, but whenever in the stroller, she drew crowds from everywhere. George quipped that they had found how to reach the masses—bring along a white-skinned baby.

Samuel and Elias toured Muharrek Island one Saturday. They sold about twenty-five books despite a mob of boys who followed them and made all kinds of trouble. A different group of boys had also caused trouble in Manama. George longed for the day when the Gospel would teach them better ways.

Samuel, Amy, George, Elias, and Yusuf celebrated the Lord's Supper together for the first time on Sunday, January 8. The five Christians were gathered together among 50,000 Muslim natives. The hymns, Scriptures, prayers, and Samuel's sermon were all in Arabic. Samuel preached on Revelation 1:9:

> I John, who also am your brother, and companion in tribulation, and in the kingdom and patience of Jesus Christ, was on the isle that is called Patmos, for the word of God, and for the testimony of Jesus Christ.

George understood several parts of the sermon. He, Amy, Elias, and Yusuf hoped Samuel would preach on the Sundays when he was present. His sermon made George hunger for the day when he would preach in Arabic like Samuel.

Elias took George on his longest tour in the second week of January. They used a donkey to carry their books and provisions. The two men took turns riding the donkey. They traveled westward along the shore where the hard sand provided a road-like surface. A belt of date palm groves lined the shore, and small villages were located about every half mile. Stops were made in all of the villages, but they discovered that very few men could read. In Senabis, Elias had a long discussion with a tailor who insisted that Christ was inferior to Muhammad. Between Senabis and the ruins of the Portuguese fort, they visited a village called Jebola. They did not sell any books there, but they were glad to find a garden where they sat down to eat their lunch, which consisted of Arab bread and some dates. They did not stay long because they wanted to reach El Bedia. In another village south of the ruins of the Portuguese fort, they sold a book containing the Gospel of Matthew and Genesis.

They turned inland and walked among the many palm groves. Visiting two more villages, they again found that people were illiterate, so they did not sell any books. They stopped at more villages when they turned to go home. As before, there were few literate people, and no books were sold. As the sun set, the two tired men arrived home. They were very satisfied with their work and having sold ten books to natives to tell the truth about God. George enjoyed many opportunities to practice his Arabic with the natives.

Writing of the route they took home, George said it ran through gardens with lofty palms on either side, a scene in stark contrast to any desolate desert a person could imagine. The tour opened George's eyes to:

how the people lived and what must be done to reach them. Evidently circulating the Scriptures will not suffice because so few can read. It must be by the spoken word that they must learn of Jesus Christ.[47]

He needed to talk fluently in Arabic because literature distribution was nearly useless. The field is opened when a person is conversant in the native language. Though the book sales were meager on the trip, if the sales continued in the future as they had been during the last three months, then the total sales in the coming year would be the largest amount ever.

The trip presented George with another insight. Several men asked him if he was a doctor. If he had been a doctor, he would have had many patients. If he could find time, along with his Arabic studies, he should pick up some basic medical knowledge and skills. They would give him more opportunities to serve the people because their own ideas of medical treatment were so crude. He could hardly fail to be an improvement. Fortunately, the number of medical personnel for the Mission was expanding, and the increase would fill the gap that he saw. He believed a doctor's presence would help break down the people's prejudices and win their hearts as in other lands.

Elias planned to depart the next week for a month-long literature distribution tour. Samuel left Bahrain for a month in mid-January for the annual Mission meeting in Busrah, Iraq. George and Yusuf remained to oversee the Bible shop and Mission house. Their oversight of the station in Samuel's absence would be a great test of their abilities to manage the station without supervision. Yusuf's presence provided the experienced Arabic speaker while Samuel was absent.

CHAPTER 15

Take Up the Work

Islam's month of daily fasting, Ramadan, began Friday, January 13. The annual observance is a duty of Muslims. Based on a lunar calendar, its start and end dates change each year. The fast begins each day at sunrise and ends at sunset. Eating and drinking are permitted throughout the night. Ramadan in 1899 gave George his first experience with it in a Muslim country. His introduction to it began with the firing of a cannon to give notice that the fast was about to start. A second cannon fired to announce the sunrise and the beginning of the fast. He believed the next thirty days would change the tone of life with "this sort of holiness which turns business topsy turvy."[1] Superficiality pervaded the observance of the fast for many of the people he walked among.

All religions struggle with outward observances of rituals versus the sincere practice of them. For instance, Ramadan 2021 began April 12. A Muslim family that my wife and I are friends with had a sign on their fireplace mantle the day before Ramadan started when we ate lunch with them. The sign had three themes listed on it: Forgiveness, Love, [Sincerity].[2] The sign reminded me of their desire to genuinely observe the fast. It is an extended time to reflect on cherished spiritual values.

In a similar vein, George participated regularly in an annual Christian week of prayer that could be observed with bare formality or with sincerity. He had fond memories of this tradition:

> I have been interested to hear of the different evangelists working in Mexico [New York] and have wondered if there have been any results after the week of prayer. We had the topics and joined our prayers with the rest of the Christian world, and my thoughts have turned to the old lecture room where so often during the week of prayer has the Holy Ghost been manifested and many saved.³

Not seeing immediate results in sharing the good news in Bahrain led George to believe the week of prayer times back home might serve another purpose:

> perhaps a preparation for me that I may have patience to wait for a slower harvest out here. It is indeed sowing beside all waters, and we can't see far ahead. We have enquirers every now and then but so far none have accepted Christ as their Savior. I am sure that a good many are convinced that we are right but are kept back by different reasons just like in America, the love of their old sins, fear of ridicule and, worse than that, persecution. It would surely come to that here, but whether they would kill a man who forsook [Islam] I don't know. I believe that God has richly blessed this mission thus far and is answering prayer every day.⁴

Before Rev. Zwemer left for Busrah, Iraq, he told George someone somewhere must be praying for him to account for his good progress in learning Arabic. This encouragement concurred with Yusuf's prediction a few days earlier that George would be conversing in Arabic soon. He sent an example of his Arabic writing to his parents that was written with an Arabic reed pen. The Bahrainis commonly wrote without a table by holding their paper in their hand and resting their arm on their knee to write. He had not perfected the method. Prayers for George continued and so did the studies with Yusuf. Together, they entertained visitors at the Bible shop and the house while Samuel was absent.

George replied to another letter from President Stryker at Hamilton College in early February. He reflected on his college experience and gave an update on his work. A football metaphor expressed his pleasure of living in Bahrain and playing on the spiritual field:

> God willing, I want to live to see a touchdown made in Arabia for the Lord Jesus Christ and if I can't carry the ball, I want to be in the interference.[5]

His optimism flourished with the great opportunity in Bahrain, Oman, and eventually throughout the Persian Gulf region:

> It is a big task the Lord has set us at, but it must be He understands what He is going to do. Arabia has never had much share in the prayers of or even the thoughts of Christians. Islam has been dodged not attacked. When once it feels the strength of a Christ-like church, it will drop so suddenly as to make us wonder at our former fears. I don't think I am deceived when I say this.[6]

Realism tempered such optimism as seen in another sports metaphor used in a letter to his college classmates, "Christianity will have no walk-over in Arabia, but what is the fun of playing an easy team?"[7]

The attendees at the Arabian Mission Annual Meeting in Busrah addressed the pressing matter of Rev. Barny's case of typhoid fever and the poor condition of the Muscat Mission house. Someone needed to relieve him and to actively oversee the house repairs. Who would that person be?

The members looked at each other and saw the predicament they were in with no other person remotely available except George. How could they appoint him with only four months of language training? This possibility was anticipated by the RCA Board of Foreign Missions. Its manual states:

> Missionaries should give their first and special attention to the work of acquiring accurately the language of the country to which they are sent, and, except under the pressure of very great necessity, of which the Mission shall judge, no other work should be allowed to interfere with this.[8]

Samuel described George's progress with Arabic. They also vouched for his willingness to do whatever was asked of him. After deliberating and praying, the members cast their votes and counted them. George's transfer to Muscat received a majority vote.

The phrase "majority vote" implies at least one person voted against the motion. Could Rev. Cantine have been a dissenter on the matter? His report in the October issue of *The Mission Field* described the difficult situation in Muscat following Peter Zwemer's departure and the Zwemers' furlough in the United States. Cantine moved to Muscat to fill Peter's vacancy until the Barnys could arrive. He specifically wrote about the danger of sending a new solo recruit to supervise a station before completing language training. Three months before the annual meeting vote about transferring George, Cantine unknowingly anticipated the future:

> to ask a new missionary, not yet six months on the field, to leave his study of the language and go off alone to supervise the work in the most trying of our stations, means a loss of time and risk of health which I trust no one after this will be asked to undergo.[9]

When the meetings ended, Samuel carried the instructions back to Bahrain for George to depart immediately for Muscat. He arrived in Manama on Tuesday, February 14 at 11 a.m. Samuel quickly informed

George of the vote that changed his life forever. The clear and urgent instructions stated:

> By the order of the majority vote of the mission you are to proceed to Muscat immediately to relieve or assist Mr. Barny, who is down with typhoid fever. With his consent and advice, you are to take the charge of the boys' school and the direction of the Bible work until the arrival of Mr. Cantine.[10]

The instructions reveal that someone consulted with Rev. Barny before the meeting to get his opinion of sending George to relieve him. Did he think George could manage the station and boys school? Rev. Barny had met him in India, present-day Pakistan, four months earlier. Rev. Zwemer wrote a year later after the vote:

> [George] was the only person available at the time, although it was not a pleasant task for a novice to be suddenly called to take care of a station of which he knew little more than the name.[11]

True to his nature, George readily accepted the instructions, ate a hearty lunch, packed up what he needed most, and boarded the same steamer at 3 p.m. that Samuel arrived on four hours earlier.

The hurried departure and rough weather on the first night gave George his first touch of seasickness in his travels. The weather was perfect the next two nights, and he understandably enjoyed the change. The officers on the SS *Assyria* were almost all Scotsmen and conversed freely. George witnessed for the first time the dazzling, glowing blue phosphorescence in the Gulf waters caused by phytoplankton.[12]

George started a letter to his parents on the trip and completed it after arriving in Muscat. They needed to know he had been transferred to Muscat. He also wrote to the *Auburn Seminary Review* summarizing the tour he made with Elias, mentioned above, and answering the students' question about the mission field:

First, that the need has not been exaggerated, and that [Islam] is as bad as it is painted. Second, that we have a splendid fighting chance here in Arabia, and the land is open enough so that we can enter [it] if we will. If a man never got beyond the Bahrain Islands he would have a parish of fifty thousand souls. Third, that on account of the [illiteracy] of the people they must be taught by word of mouth, and, therefore, if we are to reach them all, we must have many helpers. Fourth: that I am glad I came to Arabia, and that to me has been given a part in this struggle. I do firmly believe that the strength of Islam has been overestimated, and that if ever the church can be induced to throw her full weight against it, it will be found an easier conquest than we imagine—not but what it will cost lives, it has always been so, but I do believe that Islam is doomed.[13]

Fast forward to the twenty-first century. Many contemporary Muslims are disheartened by Islamic radicalism. Some Muslims choose to investigate other religions, including Christianity. An Iranian couple, in the United States to study, befriended my wife and me. They described displeasure with Iran's government and Islam, and eagerly wanted to know more about Jesus Christ. We warned them about the potential danger of rejection, persecution, or even death in identifying with Christ. Eventually, we prayed with them to trust in Christ for salvation. We mentored them, and I baptized the couple later. The husband's brother also came to the United States to study. He joined our Sunday Bible class, became a believer, and was baptized. Their hunger to know Jesus Christ made our task a delight.

George departed Bahrain where he encountered the initial stages of culture shock and speaking with the Bahrainis in simple Arabic sentences. He lived a rustic life with the Zwemers on the Gulf shore at Manama. Abject poverty, few healthcare options, and limited food choices surrounded him. Being a minority person challenged him for the first time in his life. He witnessed Samuel conversing, debating, and preaching in Arabic, which made him eager to do the same.

The transfer to Muscat unexpectedly fulfilled his desire to take up the work of a missionary. The future came to George sooner than he had ever dreamed. Because of his hurried transfer, the Mission's policy of a whole year of language study was compromised and dread filled his heart. George did not feel qualified for the task awaiting him in Muscat, but he chose to trust and obey God.[14]

PART IV

MUSCAT, OMAN

CHAPTER 16

An International Showdown

My brothers, Stephen and David, and I boarded our plane in Cairo, Egypt, bound for Muscat, Oman, on Thursday night, January 23, 2020. We landed in Muscat late at night, yet the modern city was alive with traffic from the airport to our hotel. Beautifully lit buildings shone like stars in the darkness. The Qaboos Grand Mosque stood out as especially magnificent. Our Uber driver talked about his family as we marveled at the passing sights.

My hotel room overlooked the large pool and the Gulf of Oman. Several anchored tankers and cargo ships graced the northern horizon in the morning sunlight when I opened the curtains. The ships reminded me of the economic prosperity and political importance of the region, and the vast changes since George had lived in the city.

Most Americans do not know where Oman is located. Forty-five years after George lived there, my dad piloted a C-87 to India in October 1944. The plane made stops in Aden, on the Omani island of Masirah, and in Karachi.[1] Dad had more pressing matters on his mind than to think about his great-uncle's missionary service in the Middle East.

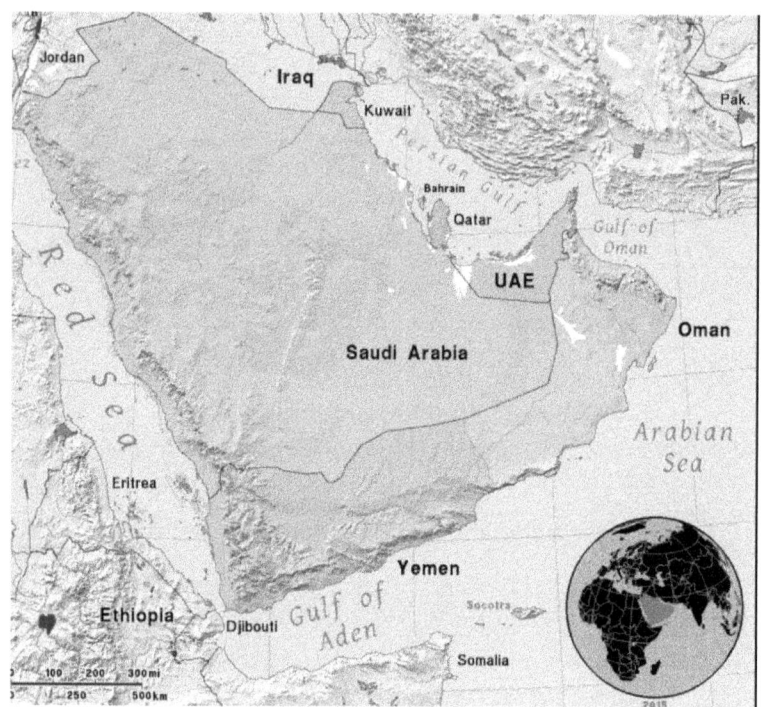

Oman to the right[2]

Oman wraps around the southeastern portion of the Arabian Peninsula. It borders Saudi Arabia to the north, Yemen on the west, and the United Arab Emirates on the northwestern border. The Gulf of Oman on the northeast and the Arabian Sea to the east and south make Oman a maritime treasure. A small peninsula separated from the rest of Oman makes up the southern part of the Straits of Hormuz, the gateway to the Persian Gulf. The eastern part of the United Arab Emirates separates the small peninsula from the majority of Oman.

Oman's ancient history includes connections to Mesopotamia, Canaan, Shebah (modern Yemen), and northern Arabia. Persians, Ethiopians, ethnic groups of Oman, Portuguese, and Turks fought over the Omani territory and maritime importance. Oman's people converted to Islam in the seventh century of the common era. The majority of Omanis identify as Ibadis, a moderate sect of Islam.[3] Oman played an important role in the African slave trade to Arabia. Slave trading contributed significantly to Oman's economy. Omani seafarers exported Islam as far as China. They had a monopoly on maritime trade until the arrival of the Portuguese at the end of the fifteenth century.

The Portuguese were the "spearhead of the western imperial transformation of the region."[4] They occupied Muscat in 1507, were expelled in 1551 by the Ottomans, and returned again in 1553. The Portuguese were expelled again in 1650. The Portuguese occupiers were harsh, and the cross of Christ became a hated symbol because of them.[5]

Western influence and control occurred again beginning in the late 1700s with the arrival of the British and their intervention against Arab piracy and slave trade. The availability of more inexpensive European goods cut into Oman's influence and power. Treaties with Britain were signed in 1798, 1822, and 1845, which officially ended Oman's slave trade economy. The British also strove to limit France's involvement in the Indian Ocean region. In the 1890s, Oman effectively became a protectorate of Britain.[6] The French opened a consulate in Muscat in 1894.[7]

The United States' relations with Oman date back to 1790 when the Boston ship *Rambler* arrived in Muscat.[8] In 1833, the two countries ratified the Treaty of Amity and Commerce.[9] The United States sent a merchant consul to Zanzabar, part of the Omani empire, in 1837. The next year, a consul took up residence in Muscat until 1845.[10] In 1840, Oman's envoy, Ahmad bin Na'aman, sailed to New York City on the *Sultanah*, the first Arab ship to visit the United States. He became the first Arab diplomat accredited to the United States. The American consulate reopened in Muscat in 1880.[11]

Muscat Harbor[12]

The Arabian Mission established its station in Muscat in 1893. Sultan Faysal bin-Turki, in power since 1888, ruled when George arrived in February 1899. The Muscat harbor and city initially looked small to George. Steep hills of dark volcanic rock surrounded the city and harbor. Entering the harbor revealed that the city and harbor were larger than they appeared from the sea. Slave trading and arms trafficking were still troublesome.[13]

The harbor faced north and was horseshoe-shaped. The water depth made it ideal as a harbor. The two heels were rock outcroppings with old Portuguese forts situated on the peaks. Al Jalali Fort is to the east and the Al Mirani Fort at the west. Below the Al Mirani Fort was a beach used by the local fishermen to land their boats. The harbor's seafront was lined from east to west with the British Consul, a private residence, Customs House, the Sultan's Bayt Al Alam Palace, and Bayt Al Barza.[14]

George heard rumors of an international crisis en route to Muscat.[15] Upon entering the harbor on February 18, he learned more details about that crisis, which had flared up two days earlier. Several British warships were anchored in the harbor: the cruiser *Eclipse*, Admiral Archibald L. Douglas' flagship, two gunboats—the *Redbreast* and *Sphinx*—and another ship, *Lawrence*, from India. Contrary to British interests and understanding of the 1891 treaty with Oman, the Sultan had violated the treaty. He planned to lease a cove near Muscat to the French for a coaling station.

When Admiral Douglas arrived, he immediately demanded that the Sultan appear onboard his ship that day. If he did not arrive onboard by 3 p.m., the forts positioned around the Muscat, and the city itself, would be bombarded by the British warships. The Sultan left his palace and boarded Admiral Douglas' ship just in time. He agreed to retract his agreement with the French.

This tense incident had cooled down when George arrived two days later. The harbor was quiet, and a week later, the *Redbreast* was the solitary warship in the harbor. George learned from telegrams he read that the incident caused no small stir in Paris.[16] This exposure to an international crisis presented him with another validation of his non-romantic view of missionary service.

CHAPTER 17

House Repairs and Slave School

George stepped out of the taxi boat from the *Assyria* in front of the Customs House to report his arrival. The sounds and smells of Muscat engulfed him. He looked up at the barren black hills of volcanic rock that surrounded the city and saw the small forts for defense. He asked for directions to the British Consulate to register and to check with the American Vice Consul, Mr. MacKirdy.

Mr. MacKirdy accompanied George to the Mission house located outside of the large wall and gate that served as the city's official land entrance. The small house stood at the foot of one of the rugged and steep hills. It had a small yard containing two wells and a half-dozen date trees. There was no courtyard. A veranda on the sunny side of the house helped moderate the interior temperature and proved a refuge at night when the hot wind forced the occupants from the roof.

When George and Mr. MacKirdy reached the house, Rev. and Mrs. Barny were in bed convalescing. Fred had typhoid fever and Margaret suffered with malaria. Part of the house wall had fallen down, and the repairs were nearly at a standstill because of Fred's physical weakness. The Barnys were obliged to live in one room of the house crammed with most of their furniture. There was no room in the house for George to use. Fortunately, Mr. MacKirdy kindly invited him to stay at his house, and he did for a week.[1]

Besides Mr. MacKirdy, the British Political Agent, Major C. G. F. Fagan, and his wife, and the French Vice Consul, Monsieur Paul Ottavi, lived in the city. These people had shown extreme kindness to the Barnys during their sicknesses, doing all they could to help them.

George devoted most of his first week overseeing the house repairs. The walls were ready for the roof. The Omanis had a particular way of roofing a house. First, they laid rafters from wall to wall that were spaced nine inches to a foot apart. On the rafters, they fastened bamboo strips in different patterns. Over the bamboo strips, they put two layers of coarse matting. On the matting, they laid small stones with mud followed by a second layer with mortar. Finally, they plastered and oiled the roof. The walls were built about a foot above the roof, creating a low parapet. George had to constantly supervise the workers to get much work done because they seemed to loiter a lot. Everything about the house was crooked. What surprised him the most was the durability of the walls because they would not have endured the rains and frosts in the United States.

While the house repairs continued, George also oversaw the Rescued Slave Boys School, supervising eighteen boys and their teacher. Peter Zwemer started the school in 1896 after the British had rescued them from slave traders. The African boys were given English names and ranged in ages from nine for little Adrian to fourteen or fifteen for James, Samuel, and John. Solomon, Isaac, and Philip were three other boys. Their mother language was Swahili. They were typical children and youths, full of life and fun and ready for mischief. One of them was nearly blind, another had always been sickly, and a third was too mentally challenged to learn in school. The rest were bright and capable. They received a Western education in English, math, geography, reading, and Bible lessons. They learned Christian songs, did chores, and the older ones learned carpentry and typesetting.

Soon after George arrived, a cousin of the Sultan visited the school, and the boys entertained him with their singing. He was impressed with their performance, repeatedly expressing his astonishment at their skill. The boys loved to sing.[2] This man returned the next day with a friend so he could also hear the boys sing.[3] George talked about Christianity with the two men after the concert. They seemed open to his explanations. He wished he could tell them all he knew, but he told them more than he thought he could, which was not much. The men flattered George when they told him he had made great progress in Arabic for such a short amount of training.

A week after arriving in Muscat, George and the boys walked down to the harbor with the Barnys to bid them farewell before they boarded the steamer to India. The boys addressed Mr. Barny as Sahib, and Mrs. Barny as Mem Sahib, which were Arabic titles for Europeans. They started calling George Sahib, too.[4]

Later in the afternoon, George returned to Mr. MacKirdy's house to thank him for his hospitality that week and to move his belongings to the Mission house. He started his duties as house parent that evening by consoling little Isaac, who cried a long time for Mem Sahib. George now managed the station on his own.

The house repairs continued into March. Once completed, the house included two upstairs rooms. The first floor room served as the school and the boys' quarters. The school room was equipped with a new blackboard, new readers, and copy books.[5] It required George's constant attention as the school's fourth headmaster in less than a year. A headmaster is in charge of the school, like a contemporary principal. His duties included supervising the teacher's instructions and serving as quartermaster for the boys' food and clothing.

Early photo of rescued slave boys[6]

Rev. Peter Zwemer received British approval to take guardianship of fourteen rescued slave boys in 1896. It cost twenty-five dollars a year for food and clothing for each boy. Renting a building and hiring a teacher were additional expenses. A short time after the boys came under Peter's care, four more boys joined the school, bringing the total to eighteen. It was the first such school in all of Arabia. The boys were taught in English to hinder their acquaintance with Islam and its customs. They proved to be capable learners, except for the ones described above.[7]

Despite the four headmaster changes in a year, the boys made fair progress in their studies. They used a fourth level reading book and worked on long division. Geography and grammar were not serious priorities. The boys read the New Testament quite readily, which is understandable since the morning exercises after breakfast started with an hour of Bible study. The schoolteacher instructed them during the day.

The boys did nearly all the chores around the house, cooked the rice and fish, drew water for the date trees, and swept the house, yard, and surrounding streets. Following supper, the boys loved to run upstairs where they sang while George played the organ, read the Bible, and prayed with them before bedtime. They attended the Sunday worship services. At the day's end, George relished the quietness once the boys were in bed and asleep downstairs.

George said of the Muscat situation:

> We are two hands short again. A mission field is in need of constant reinforcements to fill up the ranks. The death of Rev. P. J. Zwemer…leaves a large vacancy which we hope will be filled next fall by some new workers from America. In the meantime, three or four of us beginners are endeavoring to get ready to do something by and by.[8]

Rev. Cantine planned to return to Muscat in May to replace him, so George thought he would most likely be assigned to a different station.

The reports he heard about the condition of Islam in Oman were disturbing:

> From what little I have heard so far, [Islam] in this country… is in a low state. Few attend prayers in the mosques with regularity. The fast of Ramadan was not strictly kept and indifference has taken the place of fanaticism. So much corruption is found among leading [Muslims] that it is evident Islam has no saving power. Several times I have been told that only fear of the consequences kept many from acknowledging that the Gospel is the truth. The fearful persecutions which have destroyed thousands of Christians in [Muslim] lands are not forgotten and one must be truly born again who will dare to witness [for] Christ in any [Muslim] land.[9]

The report came from the Barnys and Mr. MacKirdy, who were familiar with Oman.

Sometimes, George had visitors. He talked to two men one day about the Bible. The first one was a neighbor who took the large Arabic Bible from the table and asked him to read it. George read part of the third chapter of John in which Nicodemus learns from Jesus the necessity of being born anew to enter the kingdom of God. They talked about the meaning of the passage, and the man agreed it was the truth. As far as George could tell, the man's agreement was only mental assent. He wanted to see God's Spirit bring the change of heart to people.

The second visitor, a young man, came every day for a week to receive help reading the gospels. The man could stumble along in reading them. He seemed amazed to learn from the reading how his fellow Muslims misrepresented the Bible. George's servant reported that he found the same man in town reading the gospels by himself late one night because his father was opposed to him reading the Bible. The two visitors' interest encouraged George, but he wanted to see them openly or freely confess their reliance on the truth of the Gospel. He saw the spiritual potential in the men, but he did not see any evidence of the new birth.

Sheikhs who knew and visited Peter Zwemer when he lived in Muscat came to the house to introduce themselves to George. They spoke reverently of Bishop Thomas Valpy French, who had died in Muscat in 1891 and is buried there. He had served as an Anglican bishop in India and founded the Diocese of Lahore. After he retired from the ministry, French toured the Persian Gulf region to explore where ministry to Muslims might be established. He felt a deep concern for the Arabs' needs for the good news of Jesus Christ.[10]

George said of Peter and Bishop French, "Being dead they both are speaking still."[11] He quoted other Scriptures that buttressed his confidence. "'We are waiting for the dawn;'[12] It will come. 'In due season ye shall reap if ye faint not.'[13] 'As the mountains are round about, Jerusalem, so the Lord is round about them that fear him and will deliver them,'¹⁴ whether at Muscat or Mexico, [New York]." George's hope did not waver.

A bundle of mail from home arrived that included letters and copies of the Mexico *Independent*. He read his parents' letter twice. The newspapers contained local news of people and events like the Mexico Academy Alumni Meet, Old Maid's Conference, and sad news about William H. Hall. Mr. Hall, the African American resident barber, had died suddenly. He had lived in Mexico approximately thirty years after moving there a few years after the Civil War.¹⁵ George said of this Mexico human landmark:

> I remember he was always interested in what we boys were doing and used to ask us intelligent questions regarding our work. I am more and more surprised to hear how many people whom I never supposed ever gave me a second thought appear now quite interested. I have been wonderfully blessed in friends, I know that, and separation from them is really the only privation out here. Everything else, such as climate, food, health conditions, etc., are not enough worse to make much difference, but 'old friends are best.' I made friends at Bahrain, friends I would gladly have known better, and the way things are beginning I shall have plenty here.¹⁶

The mention of friends reminded him of Mr. MacKirdy's hospitality the first week in Muscat. He possessed a charm and was a very pleasant man, cool and self-controlled. He had served in Muscat for seventeen years, had plenty of money, and lived in a fine large house that was vastly better than the Mission house.¹⁷ Mr. MacKirdy happened to be a bachelor like George.¹⁸

George started commenting on the seasonally rising temperatures that would become horrid. He noted that on March 11, the indoor thermometer registered 85 degrees Fahrenheit all day. Muscat temperatures range between 85 and 90 degrees Fahrenheit in April. After March, the heat grows intense and placed Muscat slightly above what George called "Infernal Regions." May and June are considered especially hot and disagreeable. A short break in the extreme heat occurs around the middle of July that lasts into August. An exaggerated description of the heat in Muscat by a fifteenth-century Persian stated:

> The heat is so intense that it burned the marrow in the bones, the sword in its scabbard melted like wax, and the gems that adorned the handle of the dagger were reduced to coal. In the plains the chase became a matter of perfect ease, for the desert was filled with roasted gazelles.[19]

On a more delightful note, Mr. Cantine sent George a large basket of Baghdad oranges to feast on. Oman grew and exported dates, of which there were 120 varieties. Tasting the fresh dates makes a trip to Oman worthwhile, except they ripen during summer's extreme heat.

George witnessed a rare rainfall in March. The city receives between six to ten inches a year.[20] When it rains it pours, and since the mountains are all bare rock, extraordinarily little of the water soaks into the ground. The water rushes down the steep sides of the mountains in cascades. The large flood of water flowed behind the Mission house and inundated the street. Large hailstones accompanied the storm. The schoolboys went wild over the hailstones. They picked them up and immediately dropped them as if they were red hot. They had never touched frozen water before.

All the local streams soon filled up the dry waterway in the center of the valley, and it became a rushing river for a short time. A crowd of people gathered to watch the torrent and were amused as men tried to wade in it. About a dozen young fellows started playfully dunking one another. Then they picked out unsuspecting observers, and before the person could say anything, they were thrown into the water, clothes and all. Only one or two of the victims got angry while the onlookers, including George, laughed. His servant Ali was one of the pranksters'

HOUSE REPAIRS AND SLAVE SCHOOL

victims. He was dunked about six times. The rainstorm brought in its wake delightfully cool and pleasant temperatures.

Since George's oversight of the house repairs and school consumed most of his time, he had little time to devote to his Arabic studies. He hoped to get back to them. To his advantage, he used the Arabic he knew as much as possible in conversing with the Omanis. Hearing it spoken every day increased his comprehension and familiarity with it.

George's father back in Mexico came down with pneumonia during the winter. George eagerly waited for news that he felt better.[21] Sharing news in letters about sickness increased anxiety. He and his parents had to wait a long time to receive updates. George limited his reports of sickness to reduce his parents' anxiety about his health.

George took time out one day in the latter part of March to hike up one of the little crags behind the house. The panoramic view of the city included the harbor and the dark, barren hills surrounding Muscat. The hills formed a horseshoe whose two heels met the harbor's shores. George did not carry pad and pencil to sketch the scene for his parents, but he promised to do so on another hike. George's thoughts quickly shifted from sketching to challenges. He had to return to the house at the bottom of the crag. Once there, he wrote to ask his parents to pray for him and the boys who were so weak and so easily led into sin.

Two letters arrived from the Barnys carrying the good news that their health was rapidly improving at the Convalescent House in Kandola, India. Fred said the House met all their expectations. They planned to return to Busrah, Iraq, around the middle of April. Rev. Cantine awaited their arrival. After they reached Busrah, Cantine would sail to Muscat sometime in May.

While the Barnys were getting better, George suffered another attack of fever that lasted two days. He resorted to a tablet preparation created by David Livingstone to fight the African fevers after 1853. The tablets were called Livingstone's Rousers.[22]

A clear contrast between life on Bahrain and in Muscat became apparent to George. On the island, Rev. Zwemer tended to all aspects of the missionary work while he had almost no responsibility. Now in Muscat, George had all the responsibility, though the boys, teacher, and servant assisted with duties.

George learned the ropes of managing the station and claimed he did not have any trouble. When he had first heard about the boys school back in the United States, he had secretly hoped he would be sent to some other station because he had an aversion to school. Now that he oversaw the school, it became clear to him that he was right where God wanted him. He did not waste time with regrets about what had transpired for him. George tried to figure out how God wanted him to make the best of the situation. Looking back on his first month in Muscat, he realized a little had been accomplished, which was an understatement. The house repairs were nearly finished at a reasonable price.

George gleefully relished the two upstairs rooms for himself instead of the one small room in Bahrain. He kept himself reasonably comfortable and healthy in the house as the hotter weather arrived. The rumor around town that fevers did not thrive during the hot season relieved some of his anxiety. The daily temperature in the house hovered around 82 to 87 degrees Fahrenheit. He donned white clothing to keep himself as cool as possible in the sunlight. He considered himself fortunate living in Arabia because it was still cold in his hometown. All the news he received in the papers and letters spoke of flu, sickness, great storms, and disasters on land and sea.

George's Sunday, March 26 worship services for his small congregation consisted of the teachers, literature sellers, and the boys. He spoke slowly in English about the narrow and broad ways in Matthew 7:13-14. The small audience seemed to enjoy his message, probably because they saw his thrill to be preaching again.

His only written report about the station appeared in the quarterly publication *The Arabian Mission*. It covered the six weeks he served from February 18 to March 31. The report started by describing the unfortunate events concerning Rev. Barny's sickness, the damaged house repairs, and the absence of experienced missionaries to fill in for Rev Barny. About himself, George said:

> I had to fill the gap as best I could, after four months study of the Arabic. It serves to illustrate how small our force is in spite of the reinforcements of the past year.[23]

He devoted most of the report to the school:

> Whether the Christian influences of the last three years are to triumph must soon be determined.... The discipline and general behavior of the boys has left much to be desired, but there has been a noticeable improvement of late which I hope will prove to be permanent.... The placing of the older boys in positions where they can live usefully and independently is the problem before us now and one which will require wisdom to settle satisfactorily. More than ever, we need the prayers of God's people for this school. God has richly blessed us through this troublous quarter and our trust is in Him for the future.[24]

He concluded the report with the news that Rev. Cantine would arrive in May to take charge.

George's April letter to his parents contained entries on the 14, 20, 21, and 28 of the month. He postponed sending all the news of the month until the last week. The Muscat weather continued to be comfortable in April with the temperatures ranging from 85 to 90 degrees Fahrenheit.

He had some stomach troubles that he thought were triggered by indulging too freely in "hilna" sweets[25] and Arab coffee. Hilna production was a chief industry in the city. George figured a new diet and regularly taking quinine would heal him. Then he would stay in good shape thereafter.

Samuel Zwemer wrote derogatorily of hilna, but once a person acquired a taste for it, it was delicious, "but to the stranger, [it] smells [like] rancid butter and tastes like sweet wagon-grease."[26] My brothers and I were served the modern version of this sweet by friends. It is a dark candy-paste that did not cause any stomach problems.

George took more frequent walks or hikes than in his earlier days in Muscat. He felt more relaxed and interested in his own care. He entrusted the boys to their schoolteacher or his Arabic teacher, Yusuf, when he took these walks or hikes. One hour-long hike over the nearby mountain led him to the town of Sirbab (also Sidab or Sedab), located on a small fishing cove.[27] It had a beautiful beach. He chatted with some sailors who were from the British man-of-war anchored in the Muscat harbor.[28] They were fishing with a seine net and having a grand time.

Sidab is where my brothers and I rented a boat to deliver us to the little Cove Cemetery where George is buried. Fishing boats crowded the shore, so we climbed over the boats to get to the one operated by Muhammad. He had a struggle starting the motor, but it was not his first time finagling with the battery wires. In time, the engine started, and we were on our way. We traveled slowly out of the little harbor, passed the modern jetty, and entered the open water. The skies were blue, and the water was calm and amazingly clear.

George visited other beaches on his walks, hiked up the big wadi behind the Mission house, or walked among the gardens that were about a third of a mile from the house. The gardens contained wells and were protected by a tower and sentry. People visited the gardens in the evenings for exercise.[29] Of all the places he hiked or walked to, he found the most refreshing air by the ocean.

George heard news that the British India Company intended to start a new line of steamers that would call at ports all along the Arabian coast. He knew this meant faster communication with all parts of the Arabian coast, the expansion of trade, and more opportunities to share the Gospel. The Mission could plan additional outreaches to speak to more Arabs.

George's first two months in Muscat were history. He saw his first year with the Arabian Mission sliding by very fast. His allotted seven years of service would speed by, and his furlough in 1905 would come before he realized his work had hardly started. For some reason, he expected to move from place to place in the next four months. If this were the case, he thought the movement would break up some of the monotony of the incessant heat. After Rev. Cantine arrived in Muscat to relieve him, the Mission would most likely send him to Bahrain or Busrah to complete his Arabic studies. Around October, upon passing his language examine, George would be assigned to a Mission station, but he did not know where that would be. April gave him his first experience with the monotonous heat.

CHAPTER 18

Eyes on Calendar and Thermometer

The Arabian Mission wanted to explore more of Oman to see what could be done to carry the good news of Jesus to every part of the country. Rev. Peter Zwemer had toured some of the coast and interior during his years of service (1893-98), but his efforts were cut short when he became ill and returned to the United States.[1] The previous nine years of outreach efforts by the Mission personnel accomplished many things and fueled the desire to do more.

The accomplishments included the three Mission stations operating in Busrah, Bahrain, and Muscat; thousands of portions of the Scriptures, such as Genesis and Matthew, sold; books and tracts addressing controversial religious topics circulated; and educational materials printed by the Beirut press for use at the stations. Two medical dispensaries were in service, which had done much to disarm religious prejudice. The Gospel had been preached in houses, marketplaces, coffee shops, and on streets. Hundreds of personal conversations with Muslims discussed, debated, and explained Christian beliefs and differences with Islam.

The pressing question for the Mission was whether these efforts were done in vain since the number of converts could be counted on one hand. In spite of the few results, the Mission sought more missionary recruits and literature distributers for a larger outreach. The personnel hoped that an outpouring of the Holy Spirit would lead to more converts.

Arab visitors came to the Mission house nearly every day during the third week in April. One unidentified man, a Wali of Hasreb,[2] dropped by before returning home to say goodbye. He repeated his invitation for George to visit him during the summer. On another day, George had his first good talk in Arabic on religion. The sensation of preaching the gospel in Arabic thrilled him. Another time, two Arabs called at the house. One of them held a high position under Sultan Turki. Both men talked honestly and candidly about religious matters. George considered honest and candid to mean that the Arabs said something was deficient in Islam or they saw truth in Christian beliefs. This pleased him because honesty, in his opinion, was not a common trait among Arabs. They believed they had all the truth and there was no use investigating another view. The two men, however, admitted that they had no right to condemn George or his beliefs without first examining them, any more than George did not have the right to condemn their beliefs without investigating them.

The three men discussed the authority of the Bible and the Quran. One of the men said that Muslims believed the Bible, but George replied that this could not be true since his companion had just said he did not accept the statement in 2 Peter 1:21, "For the prophecy came not in old time by the will of man: but holy men of God spake as they were moved by the Holy Ghost." The visitors fell back on a standard Islamic argument that Christians do not have the true Gospel because it had been altered. They believed in a true, genuine Bible that had not been changed.

The discussion came to an end without George giving a reason. He reported the conversation to his parents and told them what he would have said to the men if the discussion had continued. The men's position put them in a dilemma. Were the Christian Scriptures altered before or after the time of Muhammad? If they were altered before his life, then the Quran recommended that his followers use corrupted Scriptures. If the Christian Scriptures were changed after Muhammad died, then the men were denying the well-known fact that the best manuscripts of the New Testament from which all the versions were translated had been dated by scholars from 100 to 200 years before Muhammad. Even rival Christian sects had not discovered any of the presupposed alterations. Therefore, George said their argument against the Bible was too weak to stand under cross examination.

The men had another dilemma on their hands. If they obey the Quran, they were to read and obey the Bible,[3] but if they obeyed the teachings of the Bible, they needed to abandon the Quran because it denies the death and resurrection of Jesus, his deity, and the Trinity. For George, the Bible and Quran could not both be holy Scriptures since they contradict each other on those important teachings.

George believed his parents would see on what shaky grounds Islam rested. The hardest thing in the world was to make Arab men realize their position rested on an untenable foundation. Christian workers had to repeatably explain the Christian truths to them, get them to read the Bible for themselves, and then, rely on the Holy Spirit to enlighten the people's hearts and minds to the truth.

George assumed the Arabs talked about these religious matters among themselves and, in so doing, spread the Bible's message to other Arabs. He and his fellow missionaries trusted that in time the truth would leaven the whole Arab population. He affirmed the value of the work, "The object in view is well worth our best endeavors, and I am glad to have a part in it."[4]

Many Arabs stopped at the Mission house on April 21 for what George labeled as the Feast of the Pilgrimage. Their visit consumed half of George's morning, apparently interfering with his other duties. He expected many more on the other days of the four-day feast. It is actually called the Feast of the Sacrifice, Eid-ul-Adha, celebrating Abraham's willingness to sacrifice Ishmael according to Islamic teaching. The feast is observed for four days and it comes at the end of the Hajj, the mandatory visit to Mecca by able-bodied Muslims. The Hajj commemorates Abraham's pilgrimage to Mecca after Ishmael was spared according to Islamic tradition. Muhammad reinstituted the pilgrimage.[5]

George labeled the ceremonies that took place at Mecca as idolatrous to the extreme, despite Islam's claim to worship one God and its rejection of idolatry. The reverence for the Kaaba and the Black Stone in it were idolatrous. Islam could not possibly benefit anyone very much.

George had several matters to tend to concerning a few of the schoolboys. He had to discipline five of them for misbehavior. Then James, an older one, was a bad influence on the others. One Sunday night, he ran away into the walled section of Muscat and was seen with a woman. He did not return for two days because he feared punishment. Before he returned, George spoke to the British Consul, Major Fagan. He advised George to turn James over to him because the school would not succeed with him in attendance. Major Fagan wanted to send James to Bombay (Mumbai) for service. George requested one more chance with the boy. When he arrived back at the house, James was already there. He looked insolent, but George wore out a stick on his bottom. The other older boys thought it would be best for James not to be accepted back into the school. Eventually, George sent him to Major Fagan until he could be sent to India. Sickness also visited some of the schoolboys, including venereal disease and smallpox.[6]

Rev. Cantine advised George to leave Muscat before June due to the approaching incessant heat. George claimed to be immune to fever, but that was an unfounded exaggeration. Even so, he would not leave the city for he could not leave the schoolboys alone or hand them over to the British Consul.

Oman's late spring weather began to reveal its stark contrast to the lovely spring weather in Mexico, New York. Muscat's incessant heat mounted with each passing day, even though several days were pleasantly cool. Cooler temperatures were viewed as a mixed blessing in the Persian Gulf region because fevers seemed to thrive in the coolness. The comfortable weather continued into late April, holding steady at about 85 degrees Fahrenheit. Combined with the high humidity, the temperature felt much hotter. By observing precautions such as wearing light clothing and not spending a great amount of time outside in the sunlight, the climate did not feel more dangerous than in New York. Temperatures rarely reached 90 degrees Fahrenheit in the spring in his hometown. It did get hot and humid in the summer. People took advantage of the cool, refreshing waters of Lake Ontario on those hot summer days.

George's appetite improved following the stomach ailment and at least two bouts of fever. His health was nearly back to what it had been when he first arrived in Oman. His coworkers' health was another matter. "All my helpers, David and the two Yusufs, have had [serious] attacks of fever lately, but I have gained steadily…In spite of all senses, I feel like praising God for His guidance and blessing."[7]

George penned a frank description of his duties and trials in an early June letter to his Auburn Seminary friend Rev. Leonard. P. Davidson, who had graduated the year before him.[8] Rev. Davidson forwarded the letter to the seminary for the benefit of George's other friends. The four months in Muscat had been busy ones. George dreaded the transfer to Oman because he had only four months of Arabic training and no missionary experience. The duties included overseeing house repairs; providing food, clothing, and books for the boys; doctoring the sick; preaching and teaching on Sundays; and managing the Mission finances, correspondence, interruptions from callers, and Arabic studies in the gaps between all the other duties. He had had several fevers and took quinine regularly,[9] but in spite of the fevers and stomach ailment, he had not missed a single day of work, even though he was tired and ill.[10]

"Dread" is the strongest unpleasant self-description found in George's letters. His compliance with the hasty transfer did not make him immune to a feeling of incompetence for the assignment. Compliance and dread are frequent bedfellows when it comes to receiving and following orders. Jesus' desperate prayers in the Garden of Gethsemane are an example of dread and humble submission mingled together as he sought and followed God's will. Life did not get better for George.

PART V

DEATH AND BURIAL

CHAPTER 19

A Most Grievous Blow

My wife and I received a Sunday morning call on January 28, 2007, from our Army son serving in Iraq with the 509 Parachute Infantry Regiment. His Humvee had been hit by an Improvised Explosive Device (IED). He and his team members had escaped death and were receiving medical care for their injuries in an Army hospital. The initial assessment suggested a broken jaw. Our son passed the phone to his attending physician who explained to us that our son might be transported to Germany for more skilled care. Relieved by the medical report, we marveled that modern technology gave us the opportunity to talk to our son and his doctor within hours of the IED incident.

George's parents were not as fortunate when their son became deathly ill. They learned of their son's death three days after it occurred. Rev. Cantine's telegram arrived in New York City on Thursday, June 29 for the Rev. Dr. Henry N. Cobb, the Corresponding Secretary for the Reformed Church in America's Board of Foreign Missions.[1] The message bluntly stated, "Stone Dead." It did not include any details. How should he forward the shocking news to Mr. and Mrs. Stone? He wrote a letter to their pastor, Rev. Bayless, requesting that he inform the Stones. Dr. Cobb's message stated:

> We are overwhelmed with sorrow at receiving this morning a cablegram from Arabia with the two simple words, 'Stone

dead.' This is all we know and all we can know for weeks to come.²

The news left Rev. Bayless speechless. He loved George as a spiritual son. Under his ministry, this spiritual son had given his heart to Christ. He had nurtured him in the faith for eighteen years. He knew exactly what he had to do—find the Stones and break the news in person, but where were they? Mr. Stone very likely was at his store on Main Street serving customers. Mrs. Stone could be at the house on Spring Street washing clothes, gardening, or visiting a neighbor. Wherever they were at, Rev. Bayless had to break the news to them as quickly as possible. He left his office and started his search.

Rev. Bayless found Mr. Stone at his store and asked to speak to him privately. The two men walked together to the house where he met Mrs. Stone outside hanging clean, wet laundry. She saw her husband's distraught expression and knew something serious troubled him. Without saying anything, he turned to Rev. Bayless, who gently announced that the Arabian Mission's headquarters had informed him that George had died. Mr. Stone quickly moved to support his wife as her face turned pale with the shocking news.

Rev. Bayless asked that they might go into the house to talk. He could not share any details about the death because there were none. He maintained his composure as they all wondered what could have happened, and why. After the Stones shed many tears, he offered to plan a memorial service for Sunday. The Stones tearfully looked at each other and nodded their approval. Rev. Bayless prayed with them, hugged them, and departed to fulfill the unexpected task of organizing the special community service for Sunday evening, July 2. The news of George's death quickly spread through Mexico and condolences arrived at the Stones' house from around the region and across the country without anyone knowing the circumstances of his death.

Rev. Cantine was the last American to see George alive in Muscat. He wrote two letters on Friday, June 30, one to Dr. Cobb, including the death certificate, and the other one to the Stones. The letters provided the details their grieving hearts ached for so intensely. No matter how fast Cantine wrote, the letters could never arrive soon enough for the Stones and Dr. Cobb. The Stones languished in the mystery of how their son's death occurred until Thursday, August 3 when Cantine's letter arrived.

Rev. Cantine explained in his letter that he had arrived in Muscat from Busrah, Iraq, on Friday, June 9.[3] He intended to take charge of the station and give George a health furlough. He found George troubled with boils and generally run down from carrying a good deal of worry about the Rescued Slave Boys School and other matters. In spite of his condition, George seemed to manage the heat well enough, and no one thought he was seriously ill.[4] The two men took evening walks and discussed plans to do evangelistic touring, work that the weary young man was well adapted for according to Cantine.[5]

George might have sailed by steamer to a place with better medical care or climate, but the city officials had quarantined boats arriving from both north and south due to a cholera outbreak.[6] The boils on his buttocks prevented him from riding a donkey to go inland to higher and cooler temperatures, so they decided the easiest and best alternative was for him to sail in a small Omani boat up the coast a few miles to Birka, a small village with date groves. The temperature there was not much different from Muscat's, but the air quality would be better, and a change of scenery seemed to be a good idea.

An Arab acquaintance of the Mission owned a date grove in Birka and extended the invitation for George to come and stay at his place. A hut made of date branches located under the trees became George's lodging. His language teacher, Yusuf Seso, and an Omani cook accompanied them. The three men departed Thursday, June 22 at sunset.

The calm night made for a peaceful trip, and they reached Birka before sunrise.

Muscat (green line) and Barka/Birka (Red line), Oman.[7]

On Saturday, George sent a note back to Cantine requesting several personal items be sent to him. He was comfortable and remained that way until Monday morning, June 26 when he suffered a recurrence of the fever.[8] The fever passed after a couple of hours, so he ate some food at noon and afterwards laid back down and slept. The fever's return awakened him and he told Yusuf about it. The intensity grew worse, and in two hours, George became unconscious. A short time later, he died.

Yusuf informed the grove owner that George had died, and he and the cook were taking his body back to Muscat. They gathered their belongings and carried George's body to the boat, then set out for Muscat. They arrived at Muscat the next morning. Yusuf hurried to the Mission house and knocked on the door. Rev. Cantine was resting on the couch, and when he opened his eyes, Yusuf was standing in the doorway looking at him. He instinctively knew by Yusuf's facial expression what had happened to George. He asked, "Where is he?" Yusuf replied, "At the landing."

They walked silently down to the seashore, and as they approached, Cantine saw the bundle lying on the sand wrapped in a piece of old sail.[9] He knelt next to the bundle, opened it, and recognized it as George's body. Cantine's salty tears fell and mixed with the sand as he prayed to God, commending George's soul to their heavenly Father.

Cantine made the evening burial arrangements with the assistance of the British commander of the H.M.S. *Pigeon,* Lt. Edward H. Moubray.[10] He loaned the ship's steam launch with sailors to transport the coffin draped in an American flag to the Cove Cemetery. The procession following the launch included boats of the English, French, and American consuls.[11] After they pulled the boats up on the shore at the little cove, the attendees gathered around the gravesite and casket. Rev. Cantine opened his Bible and conducted the graveside service. After the benediction, Cantine and the others climbed back into the boats and returned to the harbor and their respective places of duty.

Rev. Cantine walked to the Mission house where the mood was somber among the schoolboys. Another of their Sahibs had died. Cantine gathered them together to talk to them about George, answer their questions, and pray with them. Their Sahib would never return, but he had joined the Lord Jesus and Peter Zwemer in heaven.

Reading Rev. Cantine's letter about how George had died, the dignified, international procession, and solemn burial provided some comfort for the Stones. Their son's body lay in a faraway grave on the opposite side of the Cove Cemetery from Bishop French's grave. Their two graves served as bookends for the rest of the graves.

View of Cove Cemetery from the boat. Personal Photo.

Cantine explained that the local doctor thought George's fever must have been accompanied by heat apoplexy, or heatstroke.[12] The course of his condition all seemed rather strange because Yusuf reported that the Monday temperature in Birka was not as hot as that which George lived with in Muscat. According to Cantine, George did not seem to mind the heat, but he was mistaken in stating that George had not had any fevers for several months.

Cantine wondered, along with everyone else, what would have been the outcome for George had he had access to better medical care. He answered his own question by saying no one knew. He commended Yusuf to the Stones for having loved George like a brother and doing all in his power to help him. Rev. Cantine promised Mr. and Mrs. Stone that he would see that the grave was suitably marked and preserved in accordance with the local customs. He offered to comply with any instructions they had concerning George's last resting place and the disposition of his personal belongings.

Rev. Cantine began and ended his letter addressing the great loss for the Stones and the Arabian Mission. The letter began:

> Long [before] this, I presume you have heard through Dr. Cobb that your son George has finished his brief ministry on the foreign field. Finished it with joy, though to us it is only sorrow and loss. I only knew him face to face about two weeks [June 9 – 22], but long before that, through our correspondence and through others of our mission who were privileged to know him better, I had grown to admire his character and look[ed] forward to many days to be spent as his comrade, feeling that the Lord, who had given him many gifts would greatly bless his work with us. His death is a most grievous blow to our mission. I do not see how we can get on without him, and yet God knows and into His hand we commit—tho' it be with tears—our way, its past and its future.[13]

He concluded:

> Your sorrow must indeed be keen, and more than we can here enter into, and yet there must be much of joy in it that you could offer something so precious to your Master, and of pride that your son died at the forefront of the battle with his armour on and his face to the foe. It is a glorious life to

live and more glorious death to die. With many prayers that God would comfort your hearts and feeling that you in turn will not forget this land, I remain, sincerely yours, James Cantine.[14]

CHAPTER 20

Memorial Service and Tributes

George's death remained shrouded in mystery for five weeks. Between June 29 and August 3, the Mexico community joined the Stone family in mourning and memorializing him without knowing how he had died. Rev. Bayless wrote a reply to Dr. Cobb in which he expressed his shock and disappointment with the sad and unexplained news.[1]

Rev. Bayless presided at the memorial service at the First Presbyterian Church Sunday evening, July 2.[2] He enlisted local pastors who knew George to participate in the service. A large congregation filled the sanctuary. The choir sat in the choir loft behind the pulpit and in front of the organ pipes. The front rows were occupied by George's parents; oldest brother Frederick with wife Lillie and their young sons Albert and Elmore from Dolgeville, New York; older brother Ernest and wife Jessie, also of Dolgeville; and youngest brother Harry, a student at Auburn Seminary, and many other close relatives.

The guest ministers led the opening hymn, read Psalm 23, and gave an impassioned invocation.[3] Rev. Bayless introduced the next speaker, the Rev. Edward F. Green,[4] pastor of the Parish and Hastings Presbyterian Churches. He had attended Auburn Seminary with George and gave an account of George's seminary life and influence. George's manly Christian character had won the esteem of all the students. They had elected George as a delegate to the Student Volunteer Missionary Convention in Cleveland, Ohio. The convention had confirmed for

George more than ever that his purpose was to give his life to foreign missions.

Pastor Bayless gave the next eulogy.[5] He spoke with great force and emotion in giving an incredibly beautiful and touching tribute of his young friend and his work. The message that informed him of George's death was brief and unsatisfactory because it lacked any details about the death. Yet it had to be true; otherwise, why would it have been sent? The sad news he shared with Mr. and Mrs. Stone fell upon them with crushing weight. The message startled and deeply moved the entire community with sympathetic sorrow for the family. George was one of the home-grown young men who had earned the confidence and esteem of everyone who knew him. Some of his characteristics included moral courage, consecration, simplicity, humility, and manliness. He was "a happy Christian, no misanthrope; but carried sunshine and cheer wherever he went."

Bayless told his audience that George had consecrated himself to the service of his Lord and Master at an early age. His consecration had developed into a beautiful steadfastness that could not be forgotten. He had no time or taste for dissipations by which many young men were led astray to their great detriment, if not eternally. George believed, "Life was real! Life was earnest!" Rev. Bayless felt George would concur with the sentiments from Henry Longfellow's poem "A Psalm of Life":

> Trust no future, howe'er pleasant;
> Let the dead Past bury its dead!
> Act, act in the living present!
> Heart within, and God o'erhead!

Rev. Bayless believed George had earnestly kept his eyes on the work to which he had been called—to preach the unsearchable riches of Christ.[6] George had devoted himself to preaching with great zeal as opportunity arose. He had impressed people with his fervor and sincerity of purpose. He saw himself as God's ambassador, and he had endeavored to make the most of that role. George had possessed a winsome, tactful way that had enabled him to remain true to his convictions and avoid antagonizing those who might differ with him. He had been an excellent scholar and stood among the very first in his class in college and seminary. His natural and spiritual gifts made him highly qualified for foreign missionary service. When the door opened for him to go to Arabia, he needed to enter it, even if Arabia was a most discouraging and hopeless field in which to serve. He accepted the challenge.

Rev. Bayless reminded the audience of George's farewell speech eleven months earlier. He had described Arabia, its people, their spiritual needs, and his stated purpose, God willing, to go to "the home of the False Prophet Mohammed and [to] preach the glorious gospel of the blessed God." He would have had a bright future if he had remained in the United States, but George had stood up in his consecration and bid goodbye to his friends, family, and country to go to Arabia with the "hope of leading souls out of the darkness of spiritual death into the light of the gospel of Christ."[7]

Bayless summarized George's long journey to Bahrain with the Zwemers and Margaret Rice. When they had arrived in the island country, George had plunged into his Arabic language studies. As one of the most difficult languages in the world to learn, he had made rapid progress in mastering it so that in his last letters, he had reported that he had begun to teach and preach the gospel in Arabic. Speaking of the conversations and discussions with Arabs, George had written: "Never did the Old, Old Story seem so sweet as when I could just stammer it out in Arabic."[8]

George's reports and the reports about him had fostered high hopes in the people who knew him. He had been destined to do a great work in Arabia, but his unexplained death had ended the work. Pastor Bayless concluded his presentation:

We can follow that consecrated, beautiful life no farther. The bright vision has passed. Henceforth it will be to us a beautiful memory. But it will never cease to be an inspiration to all who have seen its beauty and felt its power. 'He being dead yet speaketh.'[9] Farewell, dear brother. '*Requiescat in pace.*'[10]

The church choir passionately sang three hymns used in the farewell service before George's departure for Arabia. The Rev. T. L. Allen pronounced the benediction for a service that would be remembered for a long time by all. As the people left the sanctuary, they felt the deepest sympathy for Mr. and Mrs. Stone and George's three brothers.[11] People who did not attend the service also felt sorry for the Stones.

People read about George's death in local papers. The Pulaski, New York *Democrat* printed a brief report of George's death because one of his cousins lived there. It stated, "there is strong probability that the report [of George's death] is true." He was a "promising young man with remarkable aptness for good work." His death was a sad blow to his family and the Christian workers in the land.[12]

Two friends of the Stones sent letters to the Mexico *Independent* that were printed following the memorial service. A former pastor in Mexico, Rev. C. E. Dorr of Watertown, New York,[13] expressed deep sadness about George's passing. He viewed George as the "common heritage" of all Christian people, regardless of denomination. Rev. Dorr had anticipated future reports from him about the work he was doing in Arabia, but his death had dashed all those hopes. His letters were extremely interesting to read because George had a marvelous descriptive power, and nothing seemed to escape his notice. Finally, Rev. Dorr inquired about George's letters being printed in pamphlet form, which he thought would be very popular. Such a pamphlet was never printed.

George's Mexico friend, Rev. Arthur D. Berry, wrote the other letter. He had grown up with George, attended the Academy with him, and graduated from Syracuse University and then Drew Theological

Seminary in New Jersey. He was ordained in the Methodist Episcopal Church. He and George were both called by God to work on the frontiers of His kingdom. George's death had completed his work, but Rev. Berry's work had not yet begun. Life contained the law of sacrifice, which was necessary to make life richer. George had sacrificed his life for God's kingdom and was, thereby, a martyr and hero. He had been so patient, brave, strong, earnest, and cheerful. He made people proud of humanity.

Arthur had heard George preach once, most likely, at the Presbyterian Church in Mexico on July 12, 1896. His sermon had been based on John 12:24 about how a grain of wheat must die to produce fruit. George's death activated the law of sacrifice, "The wheat has fallen into the ground in Arabia and died, and Arabia will live in a fuller life. The law of sacrifice will be fulfilled." Rev. Arthur implored his readers:

> From his death let us all catch the glory of it, and the spirit of it. It is the glory and the spirit of sacrifice. It is the only glory we can attain to which we can take with us out into the world to come. All other glories will fade away there as the stars do in the daytime. Let us get a bit of it in all our lives.[14]

Rev. Bayless sent an announcement of George's death to *The Evangelist* soon after the memorial service. George had received copies of the publication in Arabia from his parents and enjoyed reading them. The announcement summarized Bayless' memorial remarks and ended:

> While his death, from whatever cause, is a sad blow to the [Arabian] mission, his life has been one of inspiration, and its influence will remain.[15]

The Reformed Church in America also made an announcement of George's death.

CHAPTER 21

More Tributes

Rev. Cantine's letter giving details of George's death finally arrived in Mexico on August 3. The Stones opened the envelope eagerly, yet dreadfully. They pulled out the letter, unfolded it, and read the salutation, "My dear Mr. and Mrs. Stone." The tender tone of the salutation confirmed their worst fears. Their son was dead. The envelope also included George's last written note the day after arriving in Birka. The Stones read the note and letter with many tears and realized George had not anticipated his death days before it occurred. The combination of this information with the report about the quarantining of boats at Muscat, which prevented George from leaving the city, illuminated their minds to the circumstances that were beyond anyone's control. George had died unexpectedly, mysteriously, and yet overseen by God's invisible presence.

The 2019 movie *The Last Full Measure* expresses well the contrasting feelings the Stones felt. William H. Pitsenbarger was an Air Force medic killed in action in the Vietnam War in April 1966. The first attempt for him to be awarded the Medal of Honor posthumously was denied. Thirty-five years later, a Department of Defense employee was assigned to reopen the case. This man visited William's parents in their home in Ohio. Near the end of the visit, Mr. Pitsenbarger took the investigator into William's bedroom and told him that he had been afraid and proud at the same time when his son had enlisted in the Air Force. He had been afraid of what might happen to him and also proud of what he had volunteered to do.¹ Likewise, Mr. and Mrs. Stone had been afraid and proud of their son's decision to go to Arabia. They did not want to lose their young son, but their worst fears had come true. They also knew what they needed to do with Cantine's letter.

The Stones requested that Mr. Humphries, proprietor of the *Independent*, print Rev. Cantine's letter in the newspaper for the public's benefit. The newspaper audience desperately wanted to know the circumstances of George's death. He also printed the Stones' letter of gratitude to him for printing George's letters and to the public for its many kindnesses:

> [Allow] us to express…our deep appreciation of the very many expressions of manifest Christian sympathy from dear friends and acquaintances throughout this land and other lands and also that this letter from Mr. Hickok, one of many of like character, be published…. We feel it is due the community who have manifested so deep an interest in George that these should be published in our village paper. 'Though He slay us yet will we trust Him.' In great sorrow, Mr. AND MRS. G. W. STONE.²

George's death felt like a death blow to his parents from the Lord. Great sorrow invaded their hearts. They hurt because they would not see their son again in this life. His body was buried in faraway Arabia. What could they do? What would they do? They trusted the Lord who gave them their son, trusted the One who called him to a distant land, and grasped their Savior's hand who promised to go with them through their darkest moments. While they trusted, others continued to pay tribute to their son.

The Rev. William H. Mason preached about George in the Memorial Presbyterian Church in Syracuse on July 9. He and George were classmates at Auburn Seminary. His sermon's title was, "Arabia and Its Prophet," based on John 15:13. He contrasted Muhammad's life with the Old Testament prophets and George's sacrifice. George had possessed a strong character, but a person had needed to know him to truly appreciate him. A botanist can describe a flower, but a person must see the flower for themselves to really admire it:

> The voice of [Muhammad] is craven in the presence of the heroic sacrifice of our own son. What George Stone was, not what he did, is the pledge positive of Arabia's redemption. In that far-off heathen city…he has re-won the victory of Calvary. 'Greater love hath no man than this, that a man lay down his life for his friends.' George Stone laid down his life for his friends? Nay, for his enemies, for those who hated and spurned the Christ whom he loved and preached. At the throne of God his earnest voice pleads for Arabia, and those who doubt the ultimate triumph of suffering over sin may doubt the final issue of the conflict of the Crescent with the Cross. All too short seems his life to us but God will lengthen it into an eternity of years.[3]

Mason continued with eloquent words:

> His life is symmetrical in its tragic brevity. He was one of those rare spirits who could, at any moment, strike a balance of experience and find nothing wanting. His history is only an abbreviation, to be sure, but its message is complete. With the passing of that noble life, Mecca has given way to Muscat as the hope of Arabia, George E. Stone has given his life for her redemption. His lonely grave[4] lying under the southern tropic speaks with the eternal eloquence of silence the prophetic message of salvation.[5]

George's friend offered an answer to their ageless curiosity:

> What will be the influence of his sudden death upon the world we cannot tell, but we must not forget that God advances his kingdom in the death of his saints. The world owes

the apostle Paul to the martyrdom of Stephen. It owes the matchless melody of 'In Memoriam' to the untimely death of Arthur Hallam.[6] It may yet, in the [unfathomable] providence of God, date the redemption of Arabia and the breaking down of the Muslim empire from the day of George Stone's death.[7]

Mason's glorious tribute pointed to what might happen in the future because of George's sacrifice. Everyone had to wait to see the outcome of his life and death.

Mr. Paul R. Hickok's letter to the Stones illustrated the kind of correspondence they received from a host of people. Paul had been a year behind George at Auburn Seminary. He stated the unexpected news of his friend's death shocked him and he expressed his love for George. The work of George's greatest usefulness had just begun. Death did not end George's life:

> It is not ended at all. We can see now, God wanted not so much his personal service as the force of his example and consecration to use as an incentive to others.[8]

People were better for having met George. He had possessed a sweet and beautiful spirit that reflected the spirit of his Master. Paul had been deeply touched by George's short speech at the June 1898 International Missionary Union Annual Meeting in Clifton Springs, New York.[9] He had shared George's remarks several times in his own speeches, which had encouraged many listeners. George's short speech had had a greater effect than any other that night, according to Paul. He and his Auburn friends knew how genuine George's words had been. Paul asked, and answered, why his friend should be taken away so soon:

> We can't understand all of God's ways, and it is well that we cannot. If we could, we would not have the faith to trust Him, but would try to walk always in our own knowledge.[10]

Faith meant trusting God:

> To see the sunshine thro' the rain,
> And know the promise is not vain,
> That morn shall tearless be.[11]

Paul desired to share in the Stones' deep grief. Their son had countless friends all over the United States and in other countries who would hear of his death with a sense of personal loss. That loss was, of course, greatest for the Stones. They had the sympathy of all George's friends everywhere who would be praying for God to send them:

> His own sweet Comforter to be your stay and support in this dark hour. May God bless you and us through this sorrow.[12]

The kind and sympathetic tributes reassured the Stones that they were not alone in their grief. The Department of State also sent them an official, unemotional dispatch announcing George's death. They could contact the Department for any assistance they might need.[13] George's belongings were still in Oman and Bahrain. Rev. Cantine assisted with the few belongings in Muscat. The bulk of George's possessions were with the Zwemers at the Mission station in Bahrain.

Hamilton College held a memorial service in November. The Rev. Anthony Petersen gave the eulogy in Silliman Hall, the home of the college YMCA, which George had served as president. Petersen and George had been classmates at Hamilton and Auburn. They had roomed together at Hamilton for two semesters. Rev. Petersen described his friend as:

> a college Christian *par excellence*.... The Father in Heaven was his joy, his inspiration, his very light and life.... While he ever listened to the seers and sages of truth in all ages and from all lands, there was one to whom he went for the greatest and divinest truth, and He was the Prophet and Teacher of Nazareth.... He talked as one who had walked under the

very eaves of Heaven with the God of the universe.... Many times have I seen him kneeling in prayer in his room—no doubt praying for me, and I know for his fellow students.... Splendidly equipped! Prepared for a long life's work! Death!... He never chose easy electives either in college or in life.[14]

Rev. Petersen closed with an appeal to his college audience:

And you, my young friends, if you are men of noble and large love, will find that love ofttimes makes you choose things hard. Be willing and ready to offer, if need be, your lives upon the altar of humanity's good and your brother's largest life.[15]

The Arabian Mission personnel on the mission field drafted a memorial resolution in January 1900 at its annual meeting in Busrah, Iraq:

Resolved, That we record with deep sorrow the death of our brother and comrade in the work.... His short time of service in Arabia was full of spiritual blessing to all those with whom he came in contact. He endeared himself to us all by his humility, faithfulness, tact, unselfishness, contentment and sterling character. We mourn our loss, but pray that a portion of his spirit may rest on each one of us.[16]

Rev. Cantine purchased a marble slab from Bombay (Mumbai), India for George's grave. It arrived in Muscat in 1900. The slab contained George's name and age along with the words that meant so much to him, "And he left all, rose up, and followed him."[17] Cantine wished the little Cove Cemetery was closer to the Mission house so he could visit George's grave more often. He knew, however, that "isolation of the body, living or dead, does not mean the same of the soul, and he still is often with us in our thoughts."[18] He thought of George as a unique missionary:

So bereft of his own church associations, of friends on the field, or of part in our Mission's history and development; one who had left quite so much to 'follow,' or one in whom so many have found inspiration.[19]

When Rev. Cantine visited the grave, the ocean surf provided background music and he drew strength from the memories of George's devotion. He empathized with and envisioned Mrs. Stone's tears in Mexico, New York. His confidence was renewed as he thought about God's boundless resources, George's release from his earthly service, and God's "immeasurable love that could dare to bring such sorrow to hearts that loved him."[20]

Cove Cemetery plaque. The birth date should be Sept. 1, 1873. Personal photo.

Cantine remained in Muscat and eventually closed the Rescued Slave Boys School. He found suitable work for the older boys. Almost all of the boys were placed in service at the different Mission stations or in homes of commendable nationals or foreigners. Two of the boys served on the British gunboat *Sphinx*.[21] Two died under Cantine's watch. One fell from the roof, contrary to orders, during the night while sleeping. The other boy died of cholera.[22] The boy named James, the biggest of the boys and brother to Adrian, went to an industrial school in India. He took the last name of Cantine and was later arrested for a crime. When friends read about the arrest, they thought Rev. Cantine was the guilty party.

Three of the boys—Solomon, Philip, and Isaac—requested baptism with guardians standing with them as sponsors. Cantine baptized them at the January 1900 Annual Meeting in Busrah, Iraq.[23] The Zwemers took Solomon and another boy into their house. They continued to teach the boys to read and write, trained them in household chores, and prepared them for respectable occupations. Solomon took care of the Zwemer children. After leaving the family and obtaining a job, Solomon contributed 10 percent of his income to the Reformed Church Board.[24]

With the passing of time, Rev. Cantine lost track of the boys, but he knew that some lived sincere Christian lives.[25] After the Rescued Slave Boys School was closed, the Mission opened a day school. The nephews of the Sultan attended it for several years.[26] George's four months as headmaster had not been in vain.

CHAPTER 22

The Family Carries On

A woman visited the Vietnam Traveling Memorial Wall in Santa Rosa Beach, Florida, over Labor Day weekend 2021. Her father had died in Vietnam. She told me, "I have never gotten over it." She had endured her father's death for fifty years. People learn to accept the death and the absence of the deceased without forgetting them, or they hold on to their grief as a way of keeping the person "alive."

Mrs. Stone's loss of George made it her third one since 1865. Her first husband had died less than a year after their wedding. The Stones' little four-year-old daughter Lydia Caroline had died July 25, 1873, about five weeks before George was born. Mrs. Stone never forgot Lydia. George's birth gave her a reason to keep living and carrying on. She gave birth to her fourth son, Harry, in 1875.

As a respected businessman and civic-minded resident, Mr. Stone stayed active while wearing a black band on his arm to let people know he was in a period of mourning. He and Mrs. Stone continued to participate in church activities. Mr. Stone signed the probate record of George's will in Oswego on August 16.[1]

Frederick and Ernest were partners in a dry goods store in Dolgeville, New York, northeast of Utica. Harry followed in George's footsteps at Auburn Seminary. When he graduated, he joined the YMCA as a home missionary in Watertown, New York, Springfield, Massachusetts, and the greater New York City area.[2]

The Stones purchased a headstone for George in the family plot in the Mexico cemetery that states, "George E. Stone, who died in Muscat, Arabia, June 26, 1899. Aged. 25 yrs."

Mexico, New York cemetery marker. Personal photo.

The family met together more frequently following George's death. Their oldest grandson, Albert, was almost six when he visited Mexico in the middle of August 1899. He visited the Stones, but stayed with his maternal grandmother, Mrs. Emma Becker. She hosted a party for Albert with some other little friends.[3]

Harry married Ethelyn Jessie Raymond at her parents' house in Watertown, New York, on September 20.[4] Contemporary mourning customs kept the Stones in Mexico instead of attending the small ceremony. The next week, the newlyweds and Frederick's family visited Mexico.

Mr. and Mrs. Stone visited Harry and Ethelyn in Watertown in October. They proceeded to Chazy, New York, near Lake Champlain, to visit

Sophie's relatives and friends. Leaving Chazy, they continued southwest to Dolgeville to see their two sons' families and the grandsons, Albert and Elmore.[5] They made a second trip to Chazy in November.[6]

Frederick's and Harry's families visited their parents at the Johnson Cottage on Lake Ontario in August 1900.[7] Mr. Stone attended the Syracuse Presbytery meetings in Cazenovia, New York, in September.[8] The Stones found strength to stay involved with family, friends, and community.

In August 1901, Bessie Stone visited relatives in Mexico. Her father, Walter Chester Stone, was a nephew of Mr. Stone, making Bessie his great-niece. Walter owned the Camden, New York *Advance* newspaper. Bessie spent several days with Mr. and Mrs. Stone at Lake Ontario.[9] She talked to her great-uncle and great-aunt about George, his missionary service, and death. Six years later, she married the Rev. Paul Richard Abbott. They served as Presbyterian missionaries in China from 1910 until the late 1940s. They stayed in China during World War II by moving to the western region of the country to distance themselves from the Japanese occupation force.

The Stones hosted a special guest in July 1903. The Rev. James Cantine visited them while on furlough from Muscat, Oman.[10] Rev. Cantine spoke twice in the Presbyterian Church on July 19. Harry opened the morning service with a Scripture reading and a prayer. As Mr. and Mrs. Stone and Harry listened to Rev. Cantine speak, they saw the link to their deceased son and brother. They saw the man who had examined George's body wrapped in the old piece of sail lying on the shore in Muscat. They saw the man who had arranged the dignified boat processional and burial. They saw the man who had purchased the plaque for George's grave. In the evening, the Methodist and Baptist pastors participated in the joint evening service. The church choir sang "Tarry with me, O My Savior"[11] and then Rev. Cantine gave a captivating talk on Arabia and concluded his remarks with a touching description of George's last days.[12]

Another guest visited at the Mexico Presbyterian Church on August 2. The Rev. Anthony N. Petersen, George's college and seminary friend, preached as a candidate to fill the vacancy left by Rev. Bayless' recent retirement. The church called him as its next pastor, and he began his ministry at the beginning of October. Mr. Stone assisted in welcoming guests at the reception for the Petersens two weeks later. Rev. Petersen concluded his ministry at the church in 1907.

The Rev. Samuel Zwemer visited Mexico in July 1905. He and his family were on furlough in the United States.[13] Zwemer spoke in the Wednesday evening service at the Presbyterian Church on July 26. The church was filled with an attentive audience. He spoke about "Arabia the Neglected Peninsula and the Land of Opportunity." He talked about George as one of the martyrs who had died for Arabia's salvation. Frederick and Harry returned to Mexico for the presentation.[14]

Mrs. Stone met the Zwemer family, as well as Margaret Rice, in New York City in August 1898 as the missionaries prepared to embark on their journey to Arabia. Rev. Zwemer last saw George alive on February 14, 1899, as he boarded the *Assyria* bound for Muscat. He had many recollections to share with the Stones during their short visit together. Zwemer could empathize with the Stones in their grief. The year before in 1904, Samuel and Amy's two daughters, Katarina and Ruth, died in Bahrain within a week of each other.[15] The Zwemers returned to the States with this weight of grief. Samuel and the Stones felt a deeper bond through their shared grief.

Mr. Stone became an insurance agent around 1900.[16] Almost two decades later, he and Sophie moved to Athenia, New Jersey, to live with Harry's family because of their declining health. Mr. Stone died January 25, 1919. Sophie died April 29, 1920. Their bodies were returned to Mexico for burial.

Harry Stone spearheaded a memorial service for George at the Athenia Reformed Church in Athenia, New Jersey, on Sunday, May 13, 1928.

He recruited the Rev. Dr. Anthony Petersen, George's college and seminary classmate, and Rev. James Cantine, to speak about George in the evening service. Harry's family had donated offering plates in memory of George to the church on Easter Sunday in April.

Rev. Petersen, pastor in Scarsboro, New York, and a chaplain at the Sing Sing Prison, spoke about George's character, athletic and scholastic abilities, and spiritual life. Rev. Cantine, who returned to the United States in 1927 with his wife, described George's aptitude in Arabic, the difficulties in overseeing the Rescued Slave Boys School, his illness, and death.[17] Their presentations introduced a new generation of Christians to George's life and service.

Frederick died in 1921 in Dolgeville. His wife Lillie died in 1956. Ernest owned the store until 1946. His wife Pauline died in 1960. He died in 1968. Harry retired from the YMCA in 1940. He and his wife moved to Mexico, New York, and lived there until their deaths in 1970 and 1979, respectively. The three brothers and their wives were buried in Mexico.

PART VI

REV. GEORGE E. STONE'S LEGACY

CHAPTER 23

His Legacy in Literature

George was quickly memorialized in Mexico, New York, and in the Arabian Mission literature. His legacy did not die, but with the passing of time, most details of his life story were lost. I became acquainted with my great-great-uncle approximately seventy-five years after his death by reading the brief tribute in *The History of the Arabian Mission*. My family knew he died as a missionary in Arabia, but details about his life, service, and death were extremely limited. By digging more extensively into old and contemporary sources, I found that George's legacy in literature reached into the twenty-first century. His literary legacy is highlighted below.

The Rev. Samuel M. Zwemer's *Arabia: The Cradle of Islam* is the first book to mention George following his death.[1] Zwemer wrote a large portion of the book in Bahrain while George lived with the Zwemers. At the time, Rev. Zwemer did not know he would include a tribute to George in the book. The dedication states, "To the 'Student Volunteers' of America, in memory of the two American Volunteers who laid down their lives for Arabia Peter J. Zwemer and George E. Stone." Peter and George were memorialized because Rev. Zwemer played a large role in the two young men going to Arabia. Their deaths cut to the core of his heart.

Chapter 34 in the book, titled "In Memoriam," contains short tributes to Peter and George after a cursory account of Kamil Abdul Messiah, a Syrian Muslim convert to Christ, who died in April 1892. He was the first Arabian Mission martyr. Zwemer also considered Peter and George martyrs. His account of George covered his birth, education, application to the Arabian Mission, ordination, journey to Bahrain, transfer to Oman, illnesses, and death. Zwemer declared him to be:

> a man of much promise; altogether a character of one piece without seam or rent. Sturdy, manly, straightforward, humble and honest to the core. He was entirely unconventional and did not know what it was to try to make a good impression. He was simply natural. With native tact and Yankee wit was joined a keen sense of duty and a willingness to prod.[2]

Zwemer's familiarity with George grew by mentoring him during their journey to Bahrain and sharing the Mission house together for three months on the island. Zwemer initiated George's Arabic studies and modeled ways to evangelize Muslims. George did not claim to be a linguist, but he worked hard at Arabic and made rapid progress with the difficult language. He possessed a splendid constitution, and Zwemer saw a long life of useful service for him. God had other plans.

George's letters from Muscat were always upbeat and showed that he grasped the situation with the Rescued Slave Boys School. He expected a transfer to Oman after completing language training, but not so early in the training. He rationalized the unexpected transfer:

> It is alright. Anything that has been prayed over as much as your decision at Busrah, must have been directed by God, and I have been under His orders for some time.[3]

George thanked God for the start in actual mission work in Oman, though he felt like a baby in the great work entrusted to him. God kept moving him along developmentally, little by little. If the Church put its full weight into reaching Muslims, the work would succeed. The conquest would be easier than imagined, but it would cost lives. Zwemer surmised, "Little did he think, perhaps, *whose* life it would first cost." The tribute closed with Rev. Richard C. Trench's poetic version of John 12:24, "The seed must die before the corn appears."[4]

The Reformed Church of America included a tribute to George in their June 1900 annual *Acts and Proceedings*. The tribute covers his background, progress in Arabic, transfer to the Muscat, remarks at the Clifton Springs missionary convention in June 1898, death, and burial in the Cove Cemetery where he awaits "the resurrection day in the land to which he gave his heart and his young and hopeful life."[5]

The Rev. Frederick Barny wrote about George and Peter Zwemer in a tribute following the death of another recruit, Rev. Henry J. Wiersum, in 1901.[6] His death confirmed George's conviction that the Mission's work would entail the loss of lives. Barny explained the toughness of the work:

> Was there not a mighty call for greater sacrifice and greater consecration for poor dark Arabia? God is plainly showing us that Arabia is not a Jericho whose walls of bigotry and pride and falsehood of more than a millennium's building are going to fall by the mere blowing of trumpets, though they are trumpets of faith, but that the conflict here is a war with Amalekites in which there needs must be sacrifices, and in which holy hands held up in prayer will shape the course of victory. Arabia is another East Africa, and we shall not enter it otherwise than through God's Acre.[7]

The phrase "God's Acre" refers to a cemetery where God's servants are buried.

The same issue of *Quarterly Letters* also reported the impact of the deaths of the three young men:

> The recent death of Mr. Wiersum…following in such quick succession the loss of Stone and Peter Zwemer, has already

stirred the hearts of a few young men to make offer of themselves for the work which those laborers had laid down.[8]

Zwemer wrote of George's death again in 1907 with the publication of *Islam: A Challenge of Faith*:

> Arabia has been rich in martyrs. Beside that of Keith-Falconer, it claims as heritage of promise the names of Bishop French, Peter J. Zwemer, George E. Stone, Harry J. Wiersum, Dr. Marion Wells Thoms and Mrs. Jessie Vail Bennett.[9]

The last five persons were members of the Arabian Mission. The "heritage of promise" is the law of the harvest. The deaths of God's servants hold promises like seeds planted into the ground that produce a harvest.

The Rev. Samuel Zwemer and his wife Amy toured the Middle East and India in the spring and summer of 1924.[10] They visited their two daughters' graves in Bahrain and then Samuel visited Muscat on May 15. He wondered if the Mission's work was worth it since the outward results seemed small. An answer came to him when he visited the Cove Cemetery. He prayed beside the graves of Bishop French, George, and Dr. Sharon Thoms and thought to himself:

> No one can read the records of these lives without being convinced that where such seed has been sown the harvest must come.[11]

The timing of the harvest is unknown until God brings it forth. The apostle Paul's admonition not to grow weary in doing good includes the promise that the harvest will be reaped at the proper time if we do not give up.[12]

Friends of the Arabian Mission asked a close, sympathetic, and qualified friend of the Mission to chronicle its history. The Rev. A. DeWitt Mason, DD, author of a well-known missionary history, agreed to take on the project.[13] He died before completing the manuscript. The

Rev. Fred Barny completed the project, and *The History of the Arabian Mission* was published in 1926.

Rev. Barny and George met on two occasions. The first time occurred in Karachi, India (Pakistan now), when Barny married Margaret Rice, who traveled with George and the Zwemers from August 17 to October 1, 1898. Their second meeting followed George's arrival in Muscat to relieve the Barnys on February 18, 1899. He is mentioned in three places in the book about the circumstances of his arrival, his oversight of the Rescued Slave Boys School, and the events leading to his death.[14] Two of George's letters are quoted. One is his report on the schoolboys and the request for prayer for them. The second quotation is his assessment of Islam and opinion that it would be doomed if the Church put its full weight into the task, even though it would cost the lives of people. George's optimism and death galvanized appeals for new recruits to join the Mission.

Two centennials were celebrated in George's hometown, Mexico, New York, in 1926: the founding of Mexico Academy and the arrival of the Stone family. George's brother Harry, cousin Rev. Warren Stone, and his Hamilton and Auburn classmate Rev. Anthony Petersen attended and participated in events. Harry served as the toastmaster of the banquet. Mrs. Eva Miller Martin, an 1891 alumna, informed the three hundred guests at the banquet:

> Three missionaries have gone out from the school: Frank Tubbs to [the country of] Mexico and South America; George Stone, who paid the supreme sacrifice in Arabia; Arthur Berry, now dean of our Methodist College in Tokyo [Japan].[15]

The other centennial celebrated the arrival in Mexico of Isaac and Lydia Stone and their first six children in November 1826. At least eighteen Stones attended the family reunion on August 18.[16] Harry and Ernest, George's two surviving brothers, along with their wives attended. George's nephew, Albert B. Stone, brought his wife Rowena and three young children, Marcia, Irwin, and Frederic (my father). Rowena attended the Academy. Her father, Charles Irwin Kingsbury, would serve as the Mexico Superintendent of Schools in 1926.

The Revs. Cantine and Zwemer published *The Golden Milestone: Reminiscences of Pioneer Days Fifty Years Ago in Arabia* in 1938. Their collection of personal reminiscences focused on the early pioneer days of the Mission. George, one of the pioneers, received mention by Rev. Cantine, who recounted details about George's last days, death, and burial.

Three missionaries, George, Bishop Thomas V. French, and Dr. Sharon Toms, were mentioned in Cantine's lovely picture of the small, sandy Cove Cemetery:

> only a few yards distant from the wide open sea, but not wider than was [French's] love for his fellow men, and now lies within sound of its ceaseless waves, a fitting accompaniment for his ceaseless prayers for the children of Ismael. Nearby two of our missionaries, George Stone and Sharon Thoms, rest from their labours, making of this lonely place a Mecca for the thoughts of those who love Arabia.[17]

Mecca, of course, is the destination for the annual Islamic Hajj or pilgrimage. The Cove Cemetery became Cantine's Mecca to reflect on the three men's labors to reach the homeland of Islam with the good news of Jesus Christ.

William A. Aiken, George's Hamilton College classmate, wrote the 1895 Class Annual Letter commemorating the fiftieth anniversary of the class' graduation. Eight graduates were alive in June 1945.[18] He reported that ten class members had entered the Christian ministry, and several were awarded doctorates. George was one of three classmates who went overseas and died: "England, Puerto Rico, Arabia claimed one each." Arabia, of course, referred to George.

The fiftieth anniversary of George's death occurred in 1949. Elizabeth M. Simpson happened to publish a history of Mexico, New York, *Mexico—Mother of Towns: Fragments of Local History,* that year. It includes several references to members of the Stone family, including George. She said the *Independent* gave its readers a broad education:

> By the publication of the editor's travel letters from England and the continent, those of G.H. Goodwin from California, Europe, and the Holy Land, of Arthur Berry from Japan, and of George E. Stone from England and Arabia, his mission field, readers…were offered a liberal education in world geography and folk ways.[19]

Mr. Humphries, proprietor of the *Independent* during George's life, was English, and he returned to his homeland more than once. Rev. Arthur Berry, George's childhood friend, served as a missionary in Japan for thirty-eight years after George died. Mrs. Simpson correctly highlighted the education in geography and folk ways contained in these men's letters.[20] George and Rev. Berry's missionary letters contained large amounts of religious material about the two very different cultures they served in.

Rev. Samuel Zwemer died a few days shy of his eighty-fifth birthday in 1952, the last of the three founders of the Arabian Mission to die. His successor at Princeton Theological Seminary, Dr. J. Christy Wilson, former missionary to Iran, published *Apostle to Islam: A Biography of Samuel M. Zwemer* that year. The book gives a broad overview of the immense role Zwemer played in founding the Arabian Mission, laboring to evangelize Muslims, and in world missions in general. As mentioned earlier, Zwemer visited the Cove Cemetery, Cantine's "Mecca," in May 1924. He found an affirmative answer to his troubling question about whether the Mission's meager results were worth the effort as he reflected at the graves of Bishop French, George, and Dr. Thoms and prayed.[21]

The passing of the last cofounder of the Arabian Mission ended one era and started a new era for the Mission. The personnel continued to faithfully serve Jesus Christ and adapted to the rapidly changing Persian Gulf region. Economic, political, and social advances in the Middle East gave Islam and its adherents' prestige, power, and promise. The advances forced the Western world to accept the renewed Muslim nationalism and give them equal footing in world affairs. These advances also led scholars, Christian and Muslim, to reevaluate Christian missions in general and the Arabian Mission in particular.

Abdal Malek K. Al-Tamīnī, a Muslim scholar, studied the Arabian Mission for his doctorate at University of Durham's School of Oriental Studies. Al-Tamīnī completed his thesis five years after the Reformed Church in America closed the Arabian Mission as a regional entity in 1973.[22] His dissertation *The Arabian Mission: A Case Study of Christian Missionary Work in the Arabian Gulf Region* covers many aspects of the Mission, Persian Gulf region, and the Mission's results.[23]

Al-Tamīnī believed the Arabian Mission chose the region because it had once been influenced by Christianity and the Christians wanted to regain it.[24] He concluded that the Mission failed to achieve its goal of evangelizing the Arabian Peninsula and seeing many converts. Al-Tamīnī gave several reasons for this failure. The missionaries were more idealistic than realistic. Second, the Mission did not understand the Muslims' attitude toward the Mission's work. Third, the Islamic leadership strongly opposed the Mission and argued against its success. Fourth, the missionaries overestimated the ignorance of the local people and concluded that it could successfully influence them. Lastly, limited staff and finances impacted the Mission's failure.[25]

These five reasons give us a basis to evaluate George's assessment of Islam sent to his friends at Auburn Seminary:

> First: that the need has not been exaggerated.... Second, that we have a splendid fighting chance here in Arabia, and the

land is open enough so that we can enter if we will…. Third: that on account of the ignorance of the people they must be taught by word of mouth, and therefore, if we are to reach them all, we must have many helpers. Fourth: that I am glad I came to Arabia, and that to me has been given a part in this struggle. I do firmly believe that the strength of Islam has been overestimated, and that if ever the Church can be induced to throw her full weight against it, it will be found an easier conquest than we imagine—not but what it will cost lives, it has always been so, but I do believe that Islam is doomed.[26]

Al-Tamīnī quoted this assessment in the context that the Mission had not thoroughly studied Islam and that it worked on the premise they would not face a competitive and similar faith. He did not think the missionaries were adequately equipped with Arabic to establish a natural bond with the people. Finally, the Mission's intermingling with the British and American officials confused the Indigenous about its religious goals.

Al Tamīnī's observations contain much truth in relationship to the pioneer days of the Mission, and George was one of the pioneers. He possessed only an intellectual knowledge of Islam when he arrived in Bahrain. He worked on learning Arabic to create a natural bond with the people. He never fully achieved this, even though the people respected his quick aptitude for the language in such a short time. He gained firsthand knowledge of the strong social bond between Islam and its people. He knew Muslims could be killed for leaving Islam. Rev. Cantine reported that Ibrahim, a literature seller and distributer for the Mission, heard from a group of men in a nearby village:

Do not think that all your efforts have been in vain—that the gospel is having no entrance into our hearts. It is not so. We know what the truth is, and where it is, but what can we do?

Guarantee us freedom from persecution and then you will see!"[27]

George's inexperience with the culture and language hindered his missionary effectiveness. He delighted in opportunities to interact with the people. His letters show his development in understanding. He lived and served happily in Bahrain and Oman. He was ready to stay a lifetime. Al-Tamīnī, however, believed George gave up due to illness and then died.[28]

The Quran mentions Jesus' name twenty-five times. What it teaches about him is at the core of why the Arabian Mission and George chose to serve in the Persian Gulf region. Islam teaches that Jesus is the Messiah, Son of Mary, and a great prophet. He worked miracles and ascended to heaven, but Islam denies that he was the Son of God or that he died and was resurrected. Al-Tamīnī acknowledged that the death of Jesus "is the most serious and difficult problem, which has been debated continuously by both Christians and Moslems."[29] He admitted that the four New Testament gospels teach that Jesus was crucified on the cross and rose from the dead.

Al-Tamīnī's purpose was not to engage in this theological controversy, but to touch on a few differences between Christianity and Islam. As a result, he failed to address the Arabian Mission's compulsion to bear witness to the eyewitness accounts of Jesus' death and resurrection as found in the New Testament and which occurred nearly six hundred years before Muhammad lived. Twenty of the twenty-seven books in the New Testament make explicit mention of Jesus' death and or resurrection.[30] Al-Tamīnī did not stress the importance of these testimonies to Jesus' death and resurrection as the compelling motivator of the Arabian Mission's missionary efforts.[31]

The Mission believed and operated in light of the New Testament testimony that Jesus died on the cross and was raised from the dead. It believed that denying Jesus' physical death on the cross struck at the heart of God's good news. Therefore, they endeavored to proclaim his death and resurrection as the basis of salvation from sins to Muslims in Arabia.

Al-Tamīnī ended his discussion of the different views about Jesus' death and resurrection by saying, "This disagreement is therefore among the difficulties which face any attempt at dialogue between the two religious communities."[32] George knew these opposing views. He held to the historic Christian position and believed God called him to proclaim that view to the Muslims. He died in Oman in support of the Mission's proclamation of the good news of Jesus Christ in word and deed.

Lewis R. Scudder's *The Arabian Mission's Story: In Search of Abraham's Other Son* (1998) is a thorough history of the Mission.[33] Scudder wrote about two things that puzzled the Mission's history and work. First, all the preaching efforts remained fruitless in any visible or conventional sense. An Indigenous church never developed. The law of the harvest did not show itself during the life of the Mission. The other surprise was the remarkable success in winning the appreciation of the local populations in Oman, southern Iraq, Bahrain, and Kuwait through medical and educational ministries. These services were one of the most startling displays of Christian philanthropy and devotion in missionary annals. Freedom of worship is enjoyed in Oman, Kuwait, and Bahrain to this day by immigrant workers, businessmen, Westerners, and non-Westerners. The ambiguity about the Mission was that the local people perceived it as the "American Mission," meaning it had a nationalistic thrust.[34] Scudder's observations support Al-Tamīnī's conclusions that the Mission failed to achieve its goal of evangelizing the Arabian Peninsula.

George is mentioned six times in Scudder's book. Scudder also quoted George's letter to his Auburn Seminary friends that illustrated the pioneers' optimism:

I do firmly believe that the strength of Islam has been overestimated, and that if ever the Church can be induced to throw her full weight against it, it will be found an easier conquest than we imagine—not but what it will cost lives, it has always been so, but I do believe that Islam is doomed.[35]

Later, Scudder captured the essence of George's legacy: "Others, like George Stone, left behind them the memory of their ardent youth and optimism."[36] Arabia was not an easy conquest in George's day, and it is not an easy conquest today, but George's optimism is a large part of his legacy. Whether the Mission saw results or not, George contributed to the pioneering efforts to penetrate the Arabian Peninsula.

Rev. Douglas Leonard served as the Director of the Al Amana Centre in Muscat from 2009-2016. In his 2013 article, "A Historical Survey of the US-Omani relations from 1790 to the Present," Rev. Leonard devotes a large portion to reviewing the history of the Arabian Mission's presence in Oman as it relates to the philanthropic and social services rendered by the United States' Protestant Christians and their sending churches. When the Reformed Church in America closed the Al Amana School in Muscat, it established the academic interfaith Al Amana Centre in 1987. Its purpose is to foster affinity, peace, and mutual understanding between Muslims and Christians. The Centre seeks to correct mutual misunderstandings through immersion programs in Oman that educate a broad spectrum of Christians from the US and Europe about Islam and Arab culture and, in turn, educate Muslims about Christianity.[37]

Leonard leaves the reader with the impression that George and the Barnys arrived in Muscat together to join Rev. Cantine. Rev. and Mrs. Barny, however, arrived in Muscat in October 1898 to replace Cantine. George arrived in February 1899 to relieve the Barnys so they could recuperate in India. They departed a week after he arrived. Once they recovered, they went to Busrah where Rev. Cantine resided. Cantine then sailed to Muscat to relieve George. They lived together for two weeks, before George went to Birka where he died. Cantine remained in Muscat for several years.[38]

Rev. Leonard reported that when he lived in Muscat, he took many groups to the:

> secluded graveyard on the rocky coast of Sidab.... I always felt [George's] story was so tragic. He likely came to Oman with little preparation for the complex task of supervising 18 recently freed slaves from Zanzibar. As a recent graduate.... He was so far away from home, probably intent on the adventure....[39]

Leonard thinks George might have contracted a disease carried by the schoolboys.[40]

A brief account of George is included in my biography of my father, *A Last Chapter of the Greatest Generation,* published in 2016.[41] George's education, decision to join the Arabian Mission, language training, and transfer to Muscat are described. A portion of Samuel Zwemer's tribute found in *The History of the Arabian Mission* is quoted.

In *D-Day Girls,* a book about the female spies who contributed to Germany's defeat in World War II, Sarah Rose wrote that the anonymous French partisans' ordinary kindnesses for downed Allied airmen to escape occupied France were "a modest, crucial heroism."[42] Likewise, George's legacy is the story of a modest but crucial hero. His pastor, Rev. Bayless, captured this core truth in his letter to Dr. Henry Cobb, "His was truly a heroic spirit ready to do & die if need be for his Lord."[43] His temporary assignment held the Oman Mission station together until Rev. Cantine arrived. It was crucial to sustain the station, allow the Barnys to leave to recuperate, and continue the schoolboys' education. The assignment became heroic for several reasons. He did his best to oversee the Mission station with only four months of language training. Rev. Cantine's arrival was delayed several weeks. George's health, especially in June, deteriorated, yet he never missed a workday while suffering with fevers and boils. In spite of Rev. Cantine's urging, he would not leave the station to avoid the oppressive heat in June. He could not leave the schoolboys and lose what had been invested in them since 1896. The mandated quarantine prevented him from leaving Muscat for better medical care elsewhere. Finally, his four months of service gave Rev. Fred and Mrs. Margaret Barny the chance to recuperate in India without the burden of overseeing the Muscat station and the Rescued Slave Boys School. In replacing them, George's four months in Muscat played a modest but crucial part in the Barnys' continued missionary work until their retirement in 1940. Their daughter Esther (Ames, following marriage in 1943) became the first child of the Mission's personnel to return, as a physician, to serve in the field from 1927 to 1945.[44]

George's legacy, as a modest but crucial hero, is woven into the fabric of the Arabian Mission's pioneering history. They are inseparable, as verified by Jerzy Zdankowski in his 2018 book *Saving Sinners, Even Moslems: The Arabian Mission (1889-1973) and Its Intellectual Roots*. George was "among the first…[whose] field work resulted in multiple encounters with Indigenous people, Muslims in the majority of cases."[45]

One of the beautiful features in George's letters is his stories of numerous encounters he and other coworkers had with Muslims. He included the names of many of them. His reports about these encounters support his ordination as an evangelist and missionary. His footprints of obedience to God's field of service leave a path for subsequent generations to follow in proclaiming the good news of Jesus Christ until the promised harvest appears. We do this by igniting our prayers for Arabia, activating our wills to befriend Muslims, and opening our mouths for our crucified Savior, the risen Son of God, even in the heartland of Islam when the opportunities are granted.

Rwandan-American author Immaculée Ilibagiza wrote, "God's message extends beyond borders," and "The love of a single heart can make a world of difference."[46] George went beyond his native borders with God's message. His love for God and people made a difference as a modest but crucial hero. Knowing his story enriches our lives and compels us to faithfully walk in his footsteps, laboring for the harvest from the seeds he sowed.

CHAPTER 24

Willing for It to Be So

George Stone's service to Arabia ended on June 26, 1899. He did not will it to be so, but he was willing for it to be so. He had resolved in his heart that whether he lived or died, he would be pleased to do either for Jesus Christ. George was mortal like everyone else:

> All men are like grass, and all their glory is like the flowers of the field.... The grass withers and the flowers fall, but the word of our God stands forever.[1]

George's mortality appeared earlier than his family and friends wanted for him. However, he relied on the word of God for his eternal hope. He trusted in the risen Savior for the forgiveness of his sins, salvation, and immortality. He possessed everlasting hope in life and death, and this hope permeated his decision to arise, leave all, and follow Christ to Arabia.

Mortality is no respecter of missionaries. George died before his twenty-sixth birthday. The details of his death paralleled those of the older missionary, Bishop Thomas V. French, who died in 1891 at the age of sixty-six. Bishop French retired from the Anglican ministry in India in 1887 due to failing health. His strong interest in Muslims while in India motivated him to learn Arabic to converse with them.

The bishop spent a year traveling in the Middle East upon leaving India for England. He surveyed the Muslim countries with an eye for missions in them before arriving home in 1888. He spent two years in England resting, visiting churches, giving speeches, and formulating a new plan to return to the Middle East. He bid his wife farewell and departed England in November 1890. He met the Revs. Zwemer and Cantine on their trip sailing down the Red Sea. He encouraged the two young missionaries as they sought a location for their first Arabian Mission station.

Bishop French arrived in Muscat, Oman, in February 1891 just as George did in 1899. In a letter to his wife, he wrote, "I cannot expect an effort like this to be easy and everything ready [at] hand. It is all pioneering work...."[2]

Oman's rising temperatures impacted French's health. He suffered with fevers and became feeble. When he regained strength in May, he sailed north to Sib in a boat without a canopy, which caused sunstroke. He lost consciousness. When he recovered sufficiently, he returned to Muscat and died May 14. He was buried in the Cove Cemetery. Like George's parents, Mrs. French did not learn the details of her husband's death until a letter arrived with the explanation.[3]

The same year French sailed for the Middle East in 1890, Scottish Presbyterian missionary Alexander Mackey died. His appeal for Christian missionaries for Arabia influenced French's travel plans. Mackey was an engineer who served in Zanzibar and Uganda from 1876-1890. He and his seven companions to Africa spoke to the Church Missionary Society Committee in England in April 1876 before departing for the field. Mackay was the youngest of the missionaries and the last to speak. He told the Committee:

> There is one thing my brethren have not said, and which I want to say. I want to remind the committee that within six months they will probably hear that one of us is dead. But, what I want to say is this. When that news comes, do not be

cast down, but send someone else immediately to take the vacant place.⁴

Mackay's realism was comparable to George's comment that he did not hold a romantic view of missionary service. Mackay's last days in 1890 began with a cold, which led to fevers and delirium. No medical help was available for relieving his symptoms, and he died after four days.⁵

The American missionary candidate, William Borden, arrived in Cairo, Egypt on January 1, 1913, to study Arabic. He had received God's call to serve Muslims in western China. Rev. Zwemer arrived in Cairo the same year to carry on his mission work. Borden, like George in Bahrain, entered the Zwemer family circle, though he lived at the YMCA. He moved into the home of a Syrian Christian to become immersed in spoken Arabic.

Borden contracted cerebral meningitis in March 1913 and died April 9 at the age of twenty-five. His mother and younger sister providentially were en route to Egypt to vacation with him.⁶ He heard they had arrived in Egypt, but they did not reach his bedside until four hours after his death. A simple funeral service was conducted in which Rev. Zwemer participated.

George and William Borden both died in their mid-twenties. Alexander Mackay died as a forty-year-old and Bishop French at sixty-six. They died far from their respective homelands doing what they were called to do. Life and immortality in Christ Jesus tempered their mortal lives. Their deaths raise questions of why they died and the purposes their deaths served. Rational explanations can only provide partial answers because we do not see or understand the big picture from God's vantage point.

The Rev. Dr. Arthur Hoyt, one of George's professors at Auburn Seminary, said following another young man's death, "There's a mystery in the cutting short of such a life, in its 'withheld completion.'"⁷ Everyone thought life's completion was withheld from George. Yet, if we stop to survey his short life, it is inappropriate to think of his life as incomplete. Consider the following roles he filled in his short and useful life: mentor, leader, follower, learner, headmaster, student, teacher, speaker, musician, football team manager, writer, supervisor for house repairs, toastmaster, preacher, pastor, Bible teacher, evangelist, missionary, linguist, farmhand, debater, essayist, humorist, volunteer, world traveler, friend, brother, and son. In all these roles as an unmarried person, it is arbitrary to label his life "incomplete."

Nineteenth-century English minister and author Bishop J. C. Ryle's opinion expressed George's thinking:

> I have what is good for me. I shall live on earth till my work is done and not a moment longer. I shall be taken when I'm ripe for heaven and not a minute before. All the powers of the world cannot take away my life until God permits. All the physicians of earth cannot preserve it when God calls me away.[8]

English poet Robert Laurence Binyon's poem, "For the Fallen," contains an insightful perspective on the young British soldiers who died in World War I:

> They shall grow not old as we that are left grow old;
> Age shall not weary them, nor the years condemn,
> At the going down of the sun and in the morning
> We will remember them.[9]

George did not grow old, nor did aging weary him. He was still remembered in the twenty-first century when Oman's Sultan, Qaboos bin Said Al Said, reigned. The Sultan was diagnosed with colon cancer in 2014 and died at the age of seventy-nine on January 10, 2020. He grew old and his cancer wearied him. When my two brothers and I arrived in Muscat thirteen days later on Thursday, January 23, the nation's flags flew at half-mast in honor of the deceased leader.

Two months later, we learned of COVID-19 and the pandemic that would weary the whole world and prevent many people from growing old. Millions of people, young and old, died. The same questions of why and for what purpose arose. Will the passing of time reveal some of the answers?

A hundred and twenty-one years after George died, my brothers and I worshiped with the Anglican Church in Muscat, Oman. The presiding priest, Rev. Chris Howitz, greeted us before the service, and we explained to him why we were visiting Oman. He told us he knew about George. We then visited a couple in their home who were engaged in business. They informed us they take groups of visitors to the Cove Cemetery and tell them about George and Bishop French.

Meeting Rev. Howitz and the couple helped me in two ways. First, it delighted me to learn George's legacy still exists in Oman.[10] People know of him and tell others about him. Second, God does not need me to keep George's legacy alive, but a full account of George's story waited to be discovered and written. I then told my brothers about my desire to write a biography of our ancestral uncle and asked them to pray for the writing of it.

Researching and writing this biography of George rewarded me in three ways. First, it provided marvelous inspiration. African American historian, author, and journalist Carter Godwin Woodson was born to former slaves in 1875, two years after George's birth. Woodson knew that many former slaves did not know very much about their heritage. He claimed that inspiration comes from knowing what one's ancestors accomplished:

> Those who have no record of what their forebears have accomplished lose the inspiration which comes from the teaching of biography and history.[11]

This kind of inspiration came to me in the early 1970s when I read about George's short life in *The History of the Arabian Mission*. This spark of inspiration eventually ignited a fire as I became acquainted with George's educational accomplishments, talents, and spiritual vitality. His letters contain a wealth of information about his world, journey to Bahrain, service in Oman, and his opinions. His modest but crucial sacrificial service used many of his gifts and talents. All of these elements inspire me to imagine the harvest yet to come. His endeavors inspire me to find ways to follow in his footsteps.

Several years before researching George's life, God gave my wife and me the privilege of helping Muslims place their trust in Jesus Christ as their Savior. George never experienced this joy. He met and shared the good news with Muslims, a few whom he thought were sincere inquirers, but he never saw an Arab receive the new birth through trusting in Christ. Knowing about George's prayers and labors for the Arabs means God is still using him by inspiring us to pray and labor in memory of him.

The idea to write biographies about Arabian Mission personnel such as George is found in Lewis R. Scudder's *The Arabian Mission's Story*. Scudder saw the great need for more research on the history of the Mission. He believed in 1998 that biographies of the Mission's personnel needed to be written, though he did not specifically mention George: "Someone must write a biography of John Van Ess.... And Paul Harrison.... There are other personalities worthy of study... many."[12] George is one of Scudder's "many." This biography is a contribution to help fulfill Scudder's appeal.

I have attempted to gather in one source additional information about George's formative years in Mexico, New York, at Hamilton College, and Auburn Seminary. The reader becomes acquainted with George's firsthand observations of the Arabian Mission's cofounder Samuel Zwemer and his family. Historical information about the Mission,

Bahrain, and Oman in George's letters reveal his important pioneering role and validate Scudder's call for more research.

Rev. Zwemer wrote in his biography of Raymund Lull that understanding a person requires knowing the person's environment—the age in which the person lived:

> We cannot understand a man unless we know his environment. Biography is a thread, but history is a web in which time is broad as well as long. To unravel the thread without breaking it we must loosen the web.[13]

George's thread added to history's expanding web in the last three decades of the nineteenth century. The age of progress was in full force and influenced his perspective. He possessed pride in his religious and cultural heritage. He saw the introduction of modern conveniences such as electricity and telephones in his hometown. He was a man of his times, as is evident in his essay contrasting Native Americans to the Germanic people. He did not see progress in the Native Americans, and this observation was the ground for his negative critique of them as a whole. He witnessed a similar kind of condition among the Arabs. He thought they would appreciate Western progress and thus feel more inclined to embrace Christianity. If he could see Bahrain and Oman today, he would be startled by their progress, surpassing the Western world in many ways.

My brothers David and Stephen next to George's grave. Personal photo.

George's arrival in Arabia held promise and potential for the Mission. He laughed heartily at the notion that living in Bahrain was a sacrifice for him, and this joy extended to his service in Muscat.[14] He died doing what he wanted to do and where he wanted to serve the Lord. He thought it was more important to joyously live where God called him to and to do what God wanted him to do. George possessed this joy as a modest but crucial hero to his dying day.

Bibliography

150 Years: Sesquicentennial Celebration of the First Presbyterian Church of Mexico, New York. n.p.: n.p., 1960.

Askew, Thomas A. and Richard V. Pierard. *The American Church Experience.* Grand Rapids, Michigan: Baker Academic, 2004.

Acts and Proceedings of the Regular Session of the General Synod of the Reformed Church in America. Vol. XIX June 1898 to June 1901. New York: The Board of Publication of the Reformed Church in America, 1901.

Adams, John Quincy. *A History of Auburn Theological Seminary 1818-1918.* Auburn, NY: Auburn Seminary Press, 1918.

Adams, John Quincy and William John Hinke (compilers). *Biographical Catalogue of Auburn Theological Seminary 1818-1918.* Auburn, NY: Auburn Seminary Press, 1918.

Al-Mousawi, Hussain Ben-Al-Seyed Yousuf Hashim. *A History of Omani-British Relations, with Special Reference to the Period 1888-1920.* Department of Modern History, University of Glasgow, PhD Thesis, 1990.

Anderson, Gerald H. "American Protestants in Pursuit of Missions: 1886-1986." *International Bulletin of Missionary Research.* July 1988. p. 98-110.

"Announcement of Rev George E. Stone." *The Evangelist.* 70.29 (1899: 18-19.

Auburn Theological Seminary (New York, NY) *General Biographical Catalogue of Auburn Theological Seminary, 1818-1918.* Auburn, NY: Auburn Seminary Press, 1918. Electronic reproduction. New York, NY: Columbia University Libraries, 2007.

Bekele, Yohannes. *Samuel Zwemer's Missionary Strategy Towards Islam.* School of Philosophy, Theology and Religion, The University of Birmingham, M. Philosophy Thesis, 2012.

Belmonte, Kevin. *Beacon-Light: The Life of William Borden (1887-1913).* Geanies House, Fearn, Ross-shire, Gr. Brit.: Christian Focus Publishing, 2021.

Bertrand C. Richardson et al. eds. *The Annual of Mexico Academy, Mexico, N.Y.* n.p.: n.p., 1889.

Church Reports, 1885. First Presbyterian Church, Mexico, New York. www.ancestry.com

Churchill, John C. ed. *History of Mexico, New York: From Landmarks of Oswego County.* Syracuse, NY: D. Mason & Co. Publishers, 1895.

Eilts, Hermann Frederick. *A Friendship Two Centuries Old: The United States and The Sultanate of Oman.* Washington, DC: Sultan Qaboos Center The Middle East Institute, 1990.

Harlow, S. Ralph. *The Life of H. Roswell Bates.* New York: Fleming H. Revell Company, 1914.

Henson, Rev. Josiah. *An Autobiography of the Rev. Josiah Henson.* London: "Christian Age" Office, 1877.

Hopper, Matthew S. "Imperialism and the Dilemma of Slavery in Eastern Arabia and the Gulf, 1873-1939." *Itinerario*. 30.3 (2006): 76-94.

Jessup, Henry H. *Setting of the Crescent and the Rising of the Cross: Kamil Abdul Messiah*. Philadelphia, PA: Westminster Press, 1898.

Leonard, Douglas. "A Historical Survey of US-Omani Relations from 1790 to the Present." *Oman and Overseas: Studies on Ibadism and Oman*. Vol. 2. Abdulrahman Al-Salimi and Michaela Hoffman-Ruf eds. New York: Georg Olms Verlag, 2013. p. 437-448.

Lovett, Richard. *James Gilmour of Mongolia: His Diaries Letters and Reports*. London, Gr. Brit.: The Religious Tract Society, 1895.

Madany, Bassam M. *The Missiology of Kamil Abdul Messiah: A Syrian Convert from Islam to Christianity*. Middle East Resources. www.notashamedofthegospel.org.

Mason, Alfred DeWitt and Frederick J. Barny. *The History of the Arabian Mission*. New York: The Board of Foreign Missions Reformed Church in America, 1926.

Pennell, T. L. *Among the Wild Tribes of the Afghan Frontier: A Record of Sixteen Years Close Intercourse with the Natives of the Indian Marches*. London, Gr. Brit.: Seeley, Service & Co., 1927.

Scudder, Lewis R. *The Arabian Mission's Story: In Search of Abraham's Other Son*. Grand Rapids, MI: Wm. B. Eerdman's Publishing Co., 1998.

Shumway, Bonnie, et.al. *Mexico: The 20th Town in the 20th Century*. Mexico, NY: A Mexico Historical Society Publication, 1996.

Simpson, Elizabeth M. *Mexico Mother of Towns*. Buffalo, NY: J. W. Clement Company, 1949.

Stone, Judson I. *A Last Chapter of the Greatest Generation: The Life and Family of Colonel Frederic A. Stone, M. D.* Lake Placid, NY: Aviva Publishing, 2016.

Tamm, Abdal-Malik Khalat. *The Arabian Mission: A Case Study of Christian Missionary Work in the Arabian Gulf Region.* Durham theses, Durham University, 1978. Available at Durham E-Theses Online: http://etheses.dur.ac.uk/3601/

The Celebration of the Centennial of the Founding of the Mexico Academy August 15-19, 1926. Mexico, NY: Alumni Association, 1927.

"The International Missionary Union 15th Annual Meeting." *The Missionary Review.* Vol. 21, Part 2. Princeton, NJ: Princeton Press, 1898.

The Student Missionary Appeal: Addresses at the Third International Convention of the Student Volunteer Movement for Foreign Missions. New York, NY: Student Volunteer Movement for Foreign Missions, 1898.

The World Factbook 2021. Washington, DC: Central Intelligence Agency, 2021. https://www.cia.gov/the-world-factbook/

Welch, Edgar Luderne. *Mexico, Oswego CO., and Vicinity: The Arbor Village.* Historical Souvenir Series No. 15. Syracuse, NY: GRIP, 1903.

Wilson, J. Christy. *Apostle to Islam: A Biography of Samuel M. Zwemer.* Grand Rapids, MI: Baker House Publishers, 1953.

Wilson, J. Christy. "The Apostle of Islam: The Legacy of Samuel Zwemer." *International Journal of Frontier Missions.* 13:4 (1996): 163-68.

Wilson, J. Christy, Jr. *The Story of Samuel Zwemer.* Pasadena, CA: Zwemer Institute of Muslim Studies. Original title, "The Legacy of Samuel Zwemer." July 1986. Reprinted by permission of the *International Bulletin of Missionary Research,* 1986.

Wilson, Ken. *Where No One Has Heard: The Life of J. Christy Wilson, Jr.* Pasadena, CA.: William Carey Library, 2017.

Winter, Ralph. "The Student Volunteers of 1886, Their Heirs, and the Year 2000." *International Journal of Frontier Missions.* 2.2 (1985): 151-180.

Zdanowski, Jerzy. *Saving Sinners, Even Moslems: The Arabian Mission (1889-1973) and Its Intellectual Roots.* Cambridge Scholars Publishing, 2018.

Zwemer, Samuel M. *A Moslem Seeker After God.* New York, NY: Fleming H. Revell Company, 1920.

Zwemer, Samuel M. *Arabia: The Cradle of Islam.* New York, NY: Fleming H. Revel Company, 1900.

Zwemer, Samuel M. *Call to Prayer.* London, Gr. Brit.: Marshall Brothers, 1923.

Zwemer, Samuel M. *Islam: A Challenge of Faith.* 2nd ed. New York, NY: Student Volunteer Movement for Foreign Missions, 1909.

Zwemer, Samuel M. *Raymund Lull: First Missionary to the Moslems.* New York, NY: Funk & Wagnalls Company, 1902.

Zwemer, Samuel M. *Report of a Visit to Mesopotamia the Persian Gulf and India.* New York, NY: The American Christian Literature Society for Moslem, 1924.

Zwemer, Samuel M. *Sketch of the Arabian Mission.* New York, NY: Reformed Church in America, Revised, 1907.

Zwemer, Samuel M. *The Disintegration of Islam.* New York, NY: Fleming H. Revell Company, 1916.

Zwemer, Samuel M. *The Glory of the Cross*. London, Gr. Brit.: Marshall, Morgan & Scott, 1938.

Zwemer, Samuel M. *The Muslim Doctrine of God*. New York, NY: Young People's Missionary Movement, 1905.

Zwemer, Samuel M. and Annie Van Sommer, eds. *Our Muslim Sisters: A Cry of Need from Lands of Darkness Interpreted by Those Who Heard It*. New York, NY: Fleming H. Revell Company, 1907.

Zwemer, Samuel M. and James Cantine. *The Golden Milestone: Reminiscences of Pioneer Days Fifty Years Ago in Arabia*. New York, NY: Fleming H. Revell Company, 1938.

Zwemer, Samuel M. and Amy E. Zwemer. *Topsy-Turvy Land: Arabia Pictured for Children*. New York, NY: Fleming H. Revell Company, 1902.

Endnotes

Preface

1. Mason, Rev. Alfred DeWitt and Barny, Rev. Frederick J., MA. *The History of the Arabian Mission.* New York, NY: The Board of Foreign Missions Reformed Church of America, 1926.
2. Wilson, J. Christy. *Apostle to Islam: A Biography of Samuel M. Zwemer.* Grand Rapids, MI: Baker Book House, 1952.
3. *A Last Chapter of the Greatest Generation: The Life and Family of Colonel Frederic A. Stone, M.D. Aviator, Doctor, Missionary and Friend to Humanity.* Lake Placid, NY: Aviva Publishing, 2016.

Introduction

1. *The History of the Arabian Mission.* p. 101.

PART I: A MAN OF OUR HOPES
Chapter 1: Growing Up in Mexico, New York

1. Elizabeth M. Simpson. *Mexico: Mother of Towns. Fragments of Local History.* Buffalo, NY: J. W. Clement Company, 1949. From the Foreword.
2. Ibid. p. 313. See also p. 203 in *Mexico: The 20th Town in the 20th Century* where populations of the town and village are combined for 3,404. Also, in *History of Mexico, New York: From Landmarks of Oswego County.* Ed. John C. Churchill. Syracuse, NY: D. Mason & Co. Publishers, 1895. www.history.rays-place.com/ny/mexico-ny.htm. Accessed 01/16/2021.
3. Ibid. p. 305-312.

4   Ibid. p. 435-436.

5   Mexico *Independent*. September 3, 1884. p. 4.

6   Personal letter from a great-grandson of Mr. Stone, and grandson of Harry Stone.

7   Ibid. January 25, 1899. p. 2. This may be Richard T. Simpson (1842-1915), a hardware businessman.

8   Ibid. February 8, 1899. p. 7.

9   Benjamin Dean Davis was a businessman, and not a relative. He was known in town as Uncle. http://sites.rootsweb.com/~nyoswego/biographies/Captainasadavis.html. Accessed August 25, 2022.

10 The details about the house were written by Harry and Ernest Stone for Mrs. Arnold (Irene) Caterson in *History of Spring Street, Mexico, New York*. Manuscript donated to the Historical Society, January 1978 by the Catersons. Personal copy, courtesy of the Mexico Museum, August 2022.

11 Isabelle Kingsbury Hart. *Family Stories for the Descendants of Charles Irwin Kingsbury & Lillian Belle Howell*. Privately printed, first written in 1953, and updated by granddaughter Ann Marion Penton, 2003-2004. p. 69. Isabelle was the oldest sister of my grandmother, Rowena Kingsbury Stone. I met Isabelle once around 1960. Isabella served at Oswego Normal School and Oswego State Teachers College until retiring in 1947. The college was renamed State University of New York at Oswego in 1948. A dormitory is named Hart Hall in her honor. A coworker of mine in Arlington, Texas, once lived in Hart Hall.

12 Rev. A. N. Petersen. "In Memory of Rev. George E. Stone." *Hamilton Literary Magazine*. November 1899. p. 104.

13 Ibid. p. 80.

14 *History of Spring Street, Mexico, New York*. p. 2.

15 Rev. Warren Sage Stone. "From Generation to Generation." An address presented September 10, 1944, First Presbyterian Church, Mexico, New York, following alterations made in the Lecture Room of the church. Descendants of Isaac Stone raised funds to cover the expenses of the remodeling.

16 *150 Years Commemorating the Sesquicentennial Celebration of the First Presbyterian Church of Mexico, New York 1810-1960*. p. 15.

17 *Independent*. July 5, 1899. p. 8. Remarks from the Memorial sermon at

the Presbyterian Church, July 2.

18 *150 Years Commemorating Celebration.* p. 11.
19 Ibid.
20 Ibid.
21 *Mexico Mother of Towns.* p. 277.
22 *Independent.* October 28, 1903. p. 1.
23 *Mexico Mother of Towns.* p. 282. Junius, nicknamed "June," was a cousin to George. He lived in Auburn, New York when George was a student at the seminary, according to his obituary in the *Independent,* February 23, 1933.
24 *Independent.* May 14, 1879. p. 2.
25 *Independent.* July 29, 1891. p. 1.
26 *Independent.* February 22, 1893. p. 4.
27 *Independent.* May 14, 1884. p. 2. Frederick is listed as the salutatorian in *The Celebration of the Centennial Anniversary of the Founding of the Mexico Academy.* Mexico, NY: Alumni Association, 1927. p. 180.
28 *The Annual of Mexico Academy.* Mexico, NY, 1889. p. 42.
29 Ibid. p. 45. *Mexico, Oswego Co., and Vicinity: 'The Arbor Village.'* Historical Souvenir Series, No. 15. Syracuse, NY: Grip, 1904. p. 78.
30 *The Annual of Mexico Academy.* Mexico, NY, 1889. p. 13, 18.
31 Ibid. "One Autumn night, in Sudbury town," p. 28. Delineation means to describe a character or oneself.
32 Ibid. p. 11. Translated: We came, we saw, we conquered. https://tapatalk.com/groups/pso/venimus-vidimus-vicimus-t36542.html. Accessed March 10, 2021.
33 Ibid. p. 11.
34 Kossuth (1802-1894) visited the United States in 1852. He was the second foreigner after Lafayette to address a Joint session of the US Congress. He spoke to the Ohio Legislature in February, and he may have influenced Lincoln for he said, "The spirit of our age is Democracy. All for the people, and all by the people. Nothing about the people without the people. That is Democracy!" https://en.wikipedia.org/wiki/Lajos_Kossuth#United_States
35 *Independent.* June 26, 1889, p. 2.

36 Ibid.

37 Ibid.

38 Ibid.

39 Ibid. September 4, 1889. p. 4.

40 Ibid. March 12, 1890. p. 4.

41 *The Annual of Mexico Academy.* Mexico, NY. 1889. p. 43.

Chapter 2: Hamilton College

1 Auburn relocated to New York City in 1939. https://auburnseminary.org/history/. Accessed January 29, 2021.

2 *Hamilton Literary Monthly.* January 1895. p. 154; Mexico *Independent.* July 3, 1878. p. 1.

3 Ibid. May 14, 1863. p. 3.

4 John Quincy Adams. *A History of Auburn Theological Seminary, 1818-1918.* Auburn, NY: Auburn Seminary Press. p. 166.

5 *Independent.* February 8, 1899. p. 7.

6 Half-Century Annalist Letters - 1895 Class Annalist's Letter - Hamilton College. https://my.hamilton.edu/about/history/half-century-annalists-letters/1895. Accessed February 15, 2021.

7 www.hamilton.edu. "College History." Accessed 1/9/2021. Football History and Records 12.5.2019 (PDF) - Hamilton College. https://athletics.hamilton.edu/documents/2020/10/19/Football_History_and_Records_12_5_2019.pdf. Accessed February 15, 2021.

8 Football History and Records 12.5.2019 (PDF) - Hamilton College. https://athletics.hamilton.edu/documents/2020/10/19/Football_History_and_Records_12_5_2019.pdf. Accessed February 15, 2021.

9 *Independent.* February 14, 1894. p. 14.

10 Rev. A. N. Petersen. "In Memory of Rev. George E. Stone." *Hamilton Literary Magazine.* 34.2. (November 1899): 101-02.

11 Ibid. p. 103-04.

12 *Independent.* March 9, 1892. p. 5.

13 Ibid. July 5, 1893, p. 1.

14 Ibid. July 26, 1893, p. 2.

15. Reformed Church in America Archive, Arabian Mission, 753, Box 1, 2, folders 15, 18, 19.
16. See my book *A Last Chapter of the Greatest Generation.* p. 201-205.
17. *Independent.* June 21, 1893. p. 3.
18. *Hamilton Literary Monthly.* 28.7: 285-291. Accessed at https://www.babel-hathi.org July 29, 2021. I have a scanned copy of a certificate written in Latin that George received for English, dated June 2, 1893, signed by President Stryker.
19. Ibid. January 24, 1894. p. 1. Class & Charter Day - 2019 Award Recipients - Hamilton College. https://www.hamilton.edu/ccd/2019-award-recipients. Accessed January 15, 2021.
20. *Independent.* July 3, 1895. p. 1.
21. Ibid.
22. "Our Geology Trip." Anonymous. Ancestry.com - U.S., School Yearbooks, 1900-1999. https://www.ancestry.com/imageviewer/collections/1265/images/1265_b880882-00185?treeid=5182761&personid=150001453887&usePUB=true&_phsrc=qlD737&_phstart=successSource&usePUBJs=true&pId=1405511378. Accessed June 17, 2021. William A. Aiken mentioned the geology trip in his 1895 Class Annualist's Letter, June 1945. Half-Century Annalist Letters - 1895 Class Annalist's Letter - Hamilton College. https://hamilton.edu/about/history/half-century-annalists-letters/1895. Accessed June 17, 2021.
23. June 27, 1895, Commencement Program. https://sparc.hamilton.edu/islandora/object/hamLibSparc%3A12358621#page/1/mode/1up
24. Ibid. *Independent.* June 12, 1895. p. 3.
25. The Hamilton College Epsilon chapter was established in 1869; the 20th college in the nation to establish a chapter, fifth in New York. Phi Beta Kappa - Home - Hamilton College. https://academics.hamilton.edu/phi-beta-kappa. Accessed July 24, 2021.
26. *Hamilton Literary Monthly.* June 1895. p. 352-53.
27. Ibid. July 17, 1895. p. 2.
28. Ibid. September 21, 1898. p. 4.
29. Ibid. October 12, 1898. p. 3. Explanations for these terms can be found at http://www.equineheritagemuseum.com/additional-information/a-glossary-of-harness-parts-related-terms. Accessed January 22, 2021.

30 Letter to President M. W. Stryker, Hamilton College, February 6, 1899. Courtesy of Hamilton College Archives.

31 Half-Century Annalist Letters - 1895 Class Annalist's Letter - Hamilton College. https://hamilton.edu/about/history/half-century-annalists-letters/1895. Accessed June 14, 2021.

32 *Presentation Holiday November 16, 1897, In the College Chapel.* Clinton, NY: The Courier Press. p. 4. https://ia800304.us.archive.org/3/items/presentationholi00hami/presentationholi00hami.pdf. Accessed July 24, 2021.

Chapter 3: Ministerial Training at Auburn Seminary

1 *Independent.* September 18, 1895. p. 2.

2 John Quincy Adams. *History of Auburn Theological Seminary, 1818-1918.* NY: Auburn Seminary Press, 1918. p. 163.

3 Ibid. p. 43. A synod is the governing body between a Presbytery and the General Assembly. See J. D. Douglas, General Ed. *The International Dictionary of the Christian Church.* Grand Rapids, MI.: Zondervan, 1978. p. 947.

4 Ibid. p. 47.

5 Ibid. p. 48.

6 Ibid. p. 155.

7 Ibid. p. 161.

8 Ibid. p. 159-160.

9 *Independent.* August 9, 1899. p. 8. From a memorial sermon preached July 27, 1899.

10 Ibid.

11 Letter to President Stryker. February 6, 1899. Courtesy of the Hamilton College Archives.

Chapter 4: Prepared for the Work of Service

1 *Independent.* January 1, 1896. p. 1.

2 The present Onondaga Hill Town Historian is a member of the church.

3 1 Timothy 4:12.

4 *Independent.* May 13, 1896. p. 6.

5 Two more preparatory meetings were Saturday, November 28, 1896, and Saturday, May 29, 1897. Other ministers officiated at the communion services because George was not ordained.

6 1 Corinthians 11:28-29 (NIV).

7 *Independent.* September 16, 1896. p. 3.

8 Church minutes dated November 4, 1896, and November 4, 1897.

9 *Independent.* July 15, 1896. p. 8.

10 Ibid. November 11, 1896. p. 4.

11 Ibid. December 30, 1896. p. 3.

12 Ibid. January 6, 1897. p. 4.

13 Ibid. April 7, 1897. p. 5.

14 *Independent.* March 9, 1865. p. 1. George's father and two uncles, Sidney and Henry, were in the draft but did not have to serve.

15 *Mexico Mother of Towns.* p. 394.

16 *Independent.* March 22, 1899. p. 5.

17 https://ia801006.us.archive.org/13/items/OceanofPDF.comTheAlchemist/_OceanofPDF.com_The_Alchemist.pdf. p. 16. Accessed August 31, 2022.

18 *Independent.* September 15, 1897. p. 3. Her name is printed as Jennie Pauline Drew, but her first name was Jessie. I knew her as Aunt Pauline.

Chapter 5: Clarity about God's Calling

1 *History of the Arabian Mission.* p. 78-79, 89-91.

2 Ibid. p. 61. See "Chapter V. The Pioneers 1889-1893" for the founding of the Mission. p. 57-80.

3 2 Chronicles; Ezekiel 27:21; Isaiah 21:13; Jeremiah 25:24; 1 Kings 10:15: Ezekiel 30:5.

4 Acts 2:11.

5 *The Arabian Mission's Story.* p. 61, n. 14.

6 J. Christy Wilson. *Introducing Islam.* New York: Friendship Press, 1975, p. 19-39.

7 Samuel M. Zwemer and James Cantine. *The Golden Milestone:*

Reminiscences of Pioneer Days Fifty Years Ago in Arabia. New York: Fleming H. Revell Company, 1938. p. 23, 26.

8   *History of the Arabian Mission.* p. 85-86.

9   Samuel Zwemer. "Prayer Answered and Prayer Sought." *The Mission Field.* 11.4 (1898): 128.

10 *Independent.* July 5, 1899. p. 5.

11 Ibid.

12 *The Student Missionary Appeal: Addresses at the Third International Convention of the Student Volunteer Movement for Foreign Missions, held at Cleveland, Ohio, February 23-27, 1898.* New York: Student Volunteer Movement for Foreign Missions, 1898. p. 544, 547, 549.

13 Ibid. p. 89-93, 402-404, 442-444.

14 George's classmate Harry N. Barstow and another student attended the conference. They reported to the students and faculty on the evening of November 15 in Willard Memorial Chapel. *The Auburn Seminary Review.* 1.6 (1897): 328.

15 S. M. Zwemer. *Arabia: The Cradle of Islam.* New York, NY: Fleming H. Revel, 1900. p. 371. Chapter XXXIV is titled "In Memoriam—Peter J. Zwemer and Geo. E. Stone." It was written within a year of George's death.

16 *Independent.* November 9, 1898. p. 6.

17 "Prof. Wilson's Report of the Cleveland Convention." *Maryville Times.* March 12, 1898. p. 5. Professor Wilson became the college's fifth president, 1901-1930. Maryville is my alma mater.

18 Ralph Winter. "The Student Volunteers of 1886, Their Heirs, and the Year 2000." *International Journal of Frontier Missions.* 2.2 (1985): p. 151ff. Gerald H. Anderson. "American Protestants in Pursuit of Missions: 1886-1986." *International Bulletin of Missionary Research*, July 1988. p. 98ff.

19 "Missionary Intelligence: The Student Volunteer Band." *Auburn Seminary Review.* 1.1 (1897): 41-42.

20 *Student's Handbook 1896-'97.* Auburn Theological Seminary. p. 19. Author's personal possession.

21 *Auburn Seminary Review.* 3.2 (1898): 105. Letter to Dr. Cobb, March 30, 1898. RCA Archive, Arabian Mission, 753, Box 1, 2, Folders 15, 18,

19.

Chapter 6: Preparing for the Mission Field

1. This is stamped in the Onondaga Hills church records and signed by the Moderator J. Hadell. The Reformed Church in America reported that George was a member of the "Cuyaga Presbytery," but the correct spelling is Cayuga.
2. *Independent*. April 13, 1898. p. 8.
3. Letter to Dr. Cobb March 30, 1898. RCA Archives, Arabian Mission, 753, Box 1-2, Folders 15, 18, 19.
4. April 21 letter to Dr. Henry N. Cobb, Corresponding Secretary for the RCA Board of Foreign Missions. RCA Archives.
5. *Independent*. April 13, 1898. p. 8.
6. Ibid.
7. S. M. Zwemer. *Arabia: Cradle of Islam*. New York: Fleming H. Revel Company, 1900. p. 372.
8. George received an invitation to speak at the Cattaraugus, Allegheny, Livingston, and Wyoming county conventions during May 23-26. April 21 letter to Dr. Henry N. Cobb, Corresponding Secretary of the RCA Board of Foreign Missions. Arabian Mission Correspondence, 1890-1898, 753 Box 1, files 18 and 19.
9. *Independent*. May 18, 1898. p. 4.
10. Ibid. p. 6.
11. *Acts and Proceedings of the Ninety-Fourth Regular Synod of the General Synod of the Reformed Church in America Convened at Asbury Park*, Volume XIX. *N.J.* New York: The Board of Publications, 1900. p. 904.
12. *Arabia: Cradle of Islam*. p. 371.
13. "International Missionary Union: Fifteenth Annual Meeting." *The Missionary Review*. Volume 21, Part 2. Princeton, NJ: Princeton Press, 1898. p. 604-610.
14. *Independent*. June 29, 1898. p. 7.
15. Passport number 3352. Found on Ancestry.com.
16. John 9:25.
17. *Independent*. August 10, 1898. p. 3.

18   Ibid. p. 1. Miller was an Auburn classmate, and Burt was a Hamilton classmate who gave a graduation Honors Oration "The New Psychology."

19   Professor Burt went on to Occidental College in Los Angeles and had a distinguished career there. See *Occidental College: The First Seventy-Five Years 1887-1962*. p. 16-17. https://ia802504.us.archive.org/18/items/OccidentalCollegeTheFirstSeventy-fiveYears1887-1962/scarch-3912.pdf. Accessed June 14, 2021.

Chapter 7: Farewell to Mexico, New York

1   *Independent*. August 17, 1898. p. 3.

2   Ibid.

3   Ibid.

4   Ibid.

5   Ibid.

6   $100 in 1898 → 2021 | Inflation Calculator. https://www.in2013dollars.com/us/inflation/1898?amount=100. Accessed January 23, 2021.

7   *Independent*. August 17, 1898. p. 3.

8   J. Christy Wilson. *Apostle to Islam: A Biography of Samuel M. Zwemer*. Grand Rapids, MI: Baker Book House, 1952. Arab World Pioneers, First digital edition 2016. "Margaret was the second woman in the Arabian Mission after Amy Zwemer, was a woman of fine features and an accomplished pianist, noted among the mission's 'homemakers,' and a sensitive evangelist in her own right." *The Arabian Mission's Story*. p. 171, note 119.

9   RMS Majestic Facts. https://web.archive.org/web/20060920074504/http:/www.du.edu/~tbjokne/rms_majestic.html. Accessed January 23, 2021.

10   *Independent*. August 17, 1898. p. 7.

PART II: JOURNEY TO ARABIA
Chapter 8: A Majestic Trip to Great Britain

1   "Spanish-American War." https://www.google.com/ammp/s/www.history.com/amp/topics/early-20th-century-us/spanish-american-war. Accessed June 23, 2021.

2 Proclamation 426—Thanksgiving Day, 1898 | The American Presidency Project. https://www.presidency.ucsb.edu/documents/proclamation-426-thanksgiving-day-1898. Accessed July 21, 2021.

3 Ibid.

4 *Independent.* October 26, 1898. p. 4. This page mentions President McKinley three times. Two of the references pertained to his Trans-Mississippi and International Exposition Tour in which he attended two peace celebrations, one in Chicago, and gave eighty-three speeches before returning to Washington, DC on October 20. He attended the "President's Day" Exposition on October 12, in Omaha, Nebraska. He officially opened the exposition on June 1. He began to talk about expansionism once the Spanish-American War was won. Robert P. Saldin. *War, the American State, and Politics since 1898.* Cambridge, Gr. Brit: Cambridge University Press, 2010, p. 44.

5 Thomas A. Askew and Richard V. Pierard. *The American Church Experience.* Grand Rapids, MI: Baker Academic, 2004, p.151ff.

6 Mexico, Oswego Co., and Vicinity. Historical Souvenir Series, No. 15. "The Arbor Village." Syracuse, NY: Grip, 1903. p. 24, 40. The photo on p. 40 includes George's mother.

7 First Presbyterian Church of Mexico, NY Records. www.ancestry.com.

8 Edward J. Smith - Titanic, Facts & Death - Biography. https://www.biography.com/historical-figure/edward-j-smith. Accessed March 20, 2021.

9 PAT 1.2 Public Domain World Maps. http.//ian.macky.net/pat.

10 *Independent.* September 21, 1898. p. 2.

11 Ibid.

12 Ibid.

13 George misspelled his name as Glenning. Rutherford, J., Glenny, Edward H. *The Gospel in North Africa in Two Parts.* London, Gr. Brit.: Percy Lund, Humphries & Co., Ltd., and The Country Press, Bradford, 1900.

14 http://www.birdiesperch.ca/about-us-and-our-bus/double-decker-facts-history/

15 *Independent.* September 21, 1898. p. 2.

16 https://www.thetemplebar.info/history.html. Accessed February 2, 2021.

17 https://www.walklondon.com/london-attractions/trafalgar-square-nelsons-column.htm. Accessed February 2, 2021.
18 *Independent.* September 21, 1898. p. 2.
19 Queen Victoria created the title Earl of Beaconsfield in 1876 for Benjamin Disraeli, England's only Jewish Prime Minister. https://www.britannica.com/biography/Benjamin-Disraeli/Conservative-leader. Accessed February 2, 2021.
20 *Independent.* September 21, 1898. p. 2.
21 Ibid.
22 The monument was created in 1761. https://www.westminster-abbey.org/abbey-commmorations/commemorations/lady-elizabeth-joseph-nightingale. Accessed February 2, 2021.
23 "For 30 years his life was spent in an unwearied effort to evangelize the native races, to abolish the desolating slave trade, of central Africa, where with his last words wrote, 'All I can add in my solitude, is, may Heaven's rich blessing come down on every one, American, English, or Turk, who will help to heal this open sore of the world.'" https://www.westminster-abbey.org/abby-commemorations/commemorations/david-livingstone. Accessed February 5, 2021.
24 *Independent.* September 21, 1898. p. 2.
25 Ibid.
26 Ibid.
27 Ibid.
28 Ibid.
29 https://londonist.com/2016/05/how-does-the-whispering-gallery-at-st-paul-s-actually-work. Accessed February 5, 2021.
30 https://www.gpsmycity.com/attractions/cheapside-3687.html. Accessed February 5, 2021.
31 My brother Brian and sister-in-law live in Crosshaven at Church Bay, east of Cork. George saw the Roche's Point Lighthouse located at the entrance to the Cork Harbor on the east side of the channel across from Crosshaven. The name Cobh (pronounced 'Cove') replaced the name Queenstown in the twentieth century.
32 *Independent.* September 21, 1898. p. 2.

33 Ibid.

34 Ibid.

35 Ibid.

36 Ibid.

37 Ibid.

38 It also served the British military and postal service. Samuel was very likely confirming their travel arrangements. https://www.britannica.com/biography/Thomas-Cook. Accessed February 9, 2021.

39 *Independent.* September 21, 1898. p. 2.

40 August 30 letter to Dr. Henry N. Cobb, Corresponding Secretary for the RCA Board of Foreign Missions. Arabian Mission, 1880-1898, 753 Box 1, files 18 and 19.

41 E. W. C. Sandes. *Military Engineer in India Volume II.* Chatham: The Institute of Royal Engineer, 1935, p. 9, 23-24. "Felix Haig certainly proved himself one of the ablest men ever produced by the Corps of Madras Engineers…and afterwards made his mark as Chief Engineer in the Central Provinces and then finally in Bengal."

42 S. M. Zwemer. "Death of General Haig, Honorary Trustee." *The Arabian Mission Quarterly Letters.* 39 (1901): 8-10. He was a catalyst for mission work among Muslims by the Church Mission Society, Wesleyans in Baghdad, and the formation of the North Africa Mission. "Christ was far more to him than any church."

43 It was published in 1896. See literary news in *The Evangelist.* 67.6 (1896): 19.

44 "Death of General Haig, Honorary Trustee." p. 8. Samuel first met General Haig in Suakim [Suakin], Sudan in January 1891.

45 *Independent.* September 21, 1898. p. 2.

46 George wrote about this tour in his September 6 letter.

47 George mentioned Cornell's defeat in 1895. Cornell lost to Trinity Hall, a Cambridge University boat. Heavy Henley History (PDF) - Cornell University Athletics. https://cornellbigred.com/documents/2013/6/26/Henley.pdf?id=5450. Accessed February 12, 2021.

Chapter 9: La Belle France

1 *Independent.* October 12, 1898. p. 3.

2   Ibid.

3   Ibid.

4   At the 1861 Salon, Leon Belly received a first class medal for the painting. "Pilgrims going to Mecca - Léon Belly." https://artsandculture.google.com/asset/kQH9MkXpGEydoA. Accessed February 12, 2021.

5   *Independent.* October 12, 1898. p. 3.

6   Ibid.

Chapter 10: Introduction to the Orient

1   Goanese definition, Oxford Dictionary on Lexico.com. https://www.lexico.com/en/definition/goanese. Also, meaning of Goanese. Lascar definition, Merriam-Webster. https://www.merriam-webster.com/dictionary/lascar. Accessed February 15, 2021. The proper term is Goans. See https://en.wikipedia.org/wiki/Goans# Accessed June 8, 2023.

2   More about slave trade below.

3   *Independent.* October 26, 1898. p. 5.

4   Ibid. Mark Twain's quote is from *Following the Equator.* https://study.com/academy/lesson/following-the-equator-summary-quotes.html. Accessed June 8, 2023.

5   Ibid.

6   https://www.britannica.com/place/Port-Said. Accessed February 20, 2021.

7   William Canton. *A History of the British and Foreign Bible Society, Vol. IV With Portraits and Illustrations.* London: John Murray, 1910. p. 417. https://archive.org/details/ahistoryofthebri00cantuoft/page/416/mode/1up. Accessed February 20, 2021. The gardens were named in honor of the French diplomat and Suez Canal developer Ferdinand de Lesseps. https://thearabweekly.com/egyptian-city-port-said-where-east-meets-west. Accessed February 20, 2021.

8   *Independent.* November 2, 1898. p. 1.

9   Ibid.

10 Ibid.

11 https://www.britannica.com/places/Aden. Accessed February 20, 2021.

12 Punkahs are fans suspended from ceilings and operated by a cord or

rope. https://www.merriam-webster.com/dictionary/punkah. Accessed February 20, 2021.
13. By Hattie Starr. Published in 1893. It is a lullaby that includes a small Black baby and its mother singing the lyrics. Today the song would be considered racist. https://www.bartleby.com/248/1469.html. Accessed February 20, 2021.
14. *Independent.* November 2, 1898. p. 1.
15. There are several explanations for the origin of the name. https://www.newworldencyclopedia.org/entry/Red_Sea. Accessed February 20, 2021.
16. *Independent.* November 2, 1898. p. 1.
17. Ibid.
18. Ibid.

Chapter 11: Hello, India

1. Jess may have been George's sister-in-law, married to his brother Ernest. If this is correct, she was Aunt Pauline to my family.
2. *Independent.* November 23, 1898. p. 7.
3. The Gardens were established in 1878. https://www.gpsmycity.com/attractions/karachi-zoological-gardens-33464.html. Accessed February 24, 2021.
4. *Independent.* November 23, 1989. p. 7.
5. Ibid.
6. Rev. William Dillon Waller, 1868-1953. *The Gospel in All Lands*, Methodist Episcopal Church Missionary Society, 1903. p. 224. https://books.google.com/books/about/the_Gospel_in_all_lands.html?id=sdhwnzpjqtgc. Accessed July 12, 2021.
7. *Independent.* November 23, 1898. p. 7.
8. *Independent.* December 14, 1898. p. 8. Letter dated October 14 and written in Bahrain.
9. The Barnys served in Muscat after their wedding for one quarter. They transferred to Busrah until 1908 when they returned to Oman. Rev. Barny later assumed the task of completing the *History of the Arabian Mission* started by Dr. Alfred DeWitt Mason, who died before its completion. See the Foreword in *History of the Arabian Mission* (1926). Lewis R. Scudder III in *The Arabian Mission's Story* (p. 171, n. 119 and

p. 528) states incorrectly that the Barnys were married October 19, probably because that is the date given in *The History of the Arabian Mission,* p. 97.

10 George referred to the Holy Trinity Cathedral. It was the largest Protestant church, but the Catholic St. Patrick's Cathedral was the largest church in the city. *History of the Arabian Mission,* p. 97. See also, "The Colonial City - Historic Karachi." http://historickarachi.weebly.com/the-colonial-city.html. Accessed March 5, 2021.

11 *Independent.* November 23, 1898. p. 7.

12 Ibid. December 14, 1898. p. 8.

PART III: BAHRAIN
Chapter 12: On the Mission Field

1 *Independent.* December 14, 1898. p. 8.

2 Ibid.

3 George attributed the quote to a Miller. I believe this was Joseph Walker Miller, an Auburn classmate.

4 https://www.worldheritagesite.org/list/Qal%27at+al-Bahrain. Accessed March 5, 2021.

5 PAT 1.2 Public Domain World Maps. http://ian.macky.net/pat

6 https://www.britannica.com/place/Bahrain/Cultural-life. Accessed March 5, 2021.

7 https://weather-and-climate.com/average-monthly-Rainfall-Temperature-Sunshine-fahrenheit,Bahrain,Bahrain. Accessed July 21, 2021.

8 Agha Muhammad Rahim Safar was the British agent in Bahrain (1893-1900). See "Britain's Native Agents in Arabia and Persia in the Nineteenth Century." https://socialsciences.exeter.ac.uk/iais/downloads/Britian_s_Native_Agents_2004.pdf. Accessed March 5, 2021.

9 *Independent.* December 14, 1898. p. 8.

10 *History of the Arabian Mission.* p. 74

11 *The Arabian Mission's Story.* p. 527.

12 *Independent.* December 14, 1898. p. 8.

13 Ibid.

Chapter 13: Arabic, Arabic, Arabic

1. Islam's "Sabbath" is Friday with a compulsory midday prayer time for adult males. However, the Quran teaches that Allah never needed rest after creating the world in six days (Quran 50:38), so Muslims go back to work. https://www.bl.uk/onlinegallery/features/sacred/wwoprayer.html. Accessed March 5, 2021. https://www.google.com/amp/s/theconversation.com/amp/what-is-the-islamic-weekend-33612. Accessed March 5, 2021.
2. *Independent.* December 14, 1898. p. 8.
3. *Independent.* December 28, 1898. p. 7.
4. *The Evangelist.* 69.35 (1898): 6. https://archive.org/details/sim_evangelist-and-religious-review_1898-09-01_69_35/page/6/mode/2up?q=rev.+george+bayless%2C+The+evangelist%2C+september+1898. Accessed March 9, 2021.
5. *Golden Milestone.* p. 34-36.
6. George's father's store sold suits priced from $2.50 to $12 each. See the ad for a sale. *Independent.* May 18, 1898. p. 7.
7. *Independent.* December 28, 1898. p. 7.
8. Ibid.
9. Aunt Lydia Maria Stone (1829-1914) remained single. She cared for her older sister Ruth Henrietta Stone (1827-1897), who lived with an inflamed spine until she died.
10. *Independent.* December 28, 1898. p. 8.
11. Al-Qatif is a town and oasis in the northeastern region of Saudi Arabia along the Persian Gulf. https://www.chamber.org.sa/sites/English/aboutkingdom/abouttheasternregion/pages/qatif.aspx. Accessed March 10, 2021.
12. *Independent.* January 4, 1899. p. 8.
13. Ibid.
14. *The Student Missionary Appeal: Addresses at the Third International Convention of the Student Volunteer Missionary Movement for Foreign Missions.* New York: Student Volunteer Movement for Foreign Missions, 1898. p. 442-444. Celal Emanet wrote of Samuel, "It is important to point out that, Zwemer's [sic] made a clear distinction between Islam and its followers; while on the one hand he rejected the religion on the other hand he welcomed and showed warmth to Muslims." Celal

Emanet. "An American Missionary to Islam: Samuel Marinus Zwemer." *The Journal of Academic Social Science.* Zil: 2, Sayi: 1 Mart 2014, p. 232. Accessed at www.archive.org March 23, 2021.

15 *Independent.* January 25, 1899. p. 2.
16 Ibid.
17 Ibid.
18 Ibid.
19 A Banian is an Indian Hindu merchant, trader, cashier, or moneychanger. "What does banian mean?" https://www.definitions.net/definition/banian. Accessed March 24, 2021.
20 *Independent.* January 25, 1899. p. 2.
21 George's November 24 letter included news on December 2. He started another letter dated November 29 that filled in some of the gaps between November 25 and 29. *Independent.* February 4, 1899. p. 7.
22 Authorized Version.
23 The muezzin is the person who calls people to prayer. The call to prayer is actually a song. https://referenceworks.brillonlone.com/entries/brill-s-new-pauly/muezzin-e811220. Accessed July 13, 2021.
24 "For many walk, of whom I have told you often, and now tell you even weeping, that they are the enemies of the cross of Christ: Whose end *is* destruction, whose God *is their* belly, and whose glory is in their shame, who mind earthly things." Authorized Version.
25 2 Timothy 3:5.
26 *Independent.* February 8, 1899. p. 7.

Chapter 14: The Awkward Squad

1 The al-Khamis Mosque. The foundation is dated to the eleventh century. The name is thought to derive from the Thursday market held near it. https://blogs.bl.uk/untoldlives/2015/12/the-ancient-mosque-of-manama.html. Accessed March 29, 2021. The blog includes photos of the minarets and the Cufic inscriptions.
2 Also spelled Kufic. It is a calligraphy form of script used for copying the Quran and another inscriptions. "Kūfic script." Britannica. https://www.britannica.com/topic/Kufic-script. Accessed March 26, 2021.
3 *Independent.* January 25, 1899. p. 2.

4   Ibid.

5   Ibid.

6   Edward Henry Palmer, M.A. (1840-1882) was a linguist and traveler of the Middle East. *A Grammar of the Arabic Language* was printed in 1874.

7   From the Preface in *Egypt's Princes: A Narrative of Missionary Labor in the Valley of the Nile* (2nd Ed.) Philadelphia: William S. Rentoul, 1865. p. 8. The Rev. Dr. Guilan Lansing (1826-92) was the father of Dr. John G. Lansing, co-founder of the Arabian Mission.

8   *Independent.* February 8, 1899. p. 7.

9   Also spelled "al-Hasa" or "al-Ahsa." It is the name of the largest groundwater-fed oasis in the world, located about 60 km inland from the Persian Gulf. "Hasa, al-." https://www.encyclopedia.com/humanities/encyclopedias-almanacs-transcripts-and-maps/hasa-al. Accessed April 3, 2021.

10 Nehemiah 4:17.

11 "Treaty of Paris ends Spanish-American War." https://www.google.com/amp/s/www.history.com/.amp/this-day-in-history/treaty-of-paris-ends-spanish-american-war. Accessed July 13, 2021.

12 James W. Fiscus. "Gun Running in Arabia: The Introduction of Modern Arms to the Peninsula, 1880-1914." (1987). *Dissertations and Theses. Paper 1624.* https://doi.org/10.15760/etd/1623.

13 Undated letter, but the mention of the impending New Year places the date in December. Courtesy of Hamilton College Archives.

14 Also spelled majlis. George used the word as a meeting place, though it can refer to a legislative assembly. https://ich.unesco.org/en/RL/majlis-a-cultural-and-social-space-01076. Accessed April 5, 2021.

15 *Independent.* March 1, 1899. p. 2.

16 Genesis 39:20-41:40.

17 Spirits that can be righteous or unrighteous. Sura 72 in the Quran is titled "The Jinn." https://insidearabia.com/djin-muslim-culture-truth-superstition. Accessed March 31, 2021.

18 *Independent.* March 1, 1899. p. 2.

19 His last name is spelled Gilmour. 1843-1891. George was probably reading *James Gilmour of Mongolia: His Diaries, Letters and Reports.* Ed.

Richard Lovett. London: The Religious Tract Society, 2nd ed., 1893.

20 *Independent.* March 1, 1899. p. 2. See Brian Hogan's exciting account of the church planting movement in modern Mongolia, *There's a Sheep in My Bathtub.* Bayside, CA: Asteroidea Books, 2008.

21 The last name is spelled "Brandee" in this letter. This might be a printing error by the newspaper.

22 *Independent.* March 1, 1899. p. 2.

23 Ibid.

24 Zwemer "had an irrepressible and aggressive personality, earnest… driving…" (p. 140). He "became a master in the art of 'Muslim controversy,' and many of the stories about him show him in this light. But to win an argument, to silence an opponent, is not to win a heart." (p. 140-41, note 33) in *The Arabian Mission's Story.*

25 For a deeper and more critical view of Zwemer's relationship to Muslims, see *The Arabian Mission's Story,* p. 189-191, n. 168.

26 *Independent.* March 1, 1899. p. 2.

27 Amos Baldwin (1831-1910) married George's aunt Julia P. Stone (b. 1831) who died in 1861; Amos married Julia's younger sister, Jane O. Stone (1839-1923). Uncle Amos was a farmer.

28 George used the word "pice," which was a coin from India. https://www.definitions.net/definition/PICE. Accessed April 6, 2021.

29 A total lunar eclipse occurred on December 27, 1898. https://moonblink.info/Eclipse/eclipse/1898_12_27. Accessed April 22, 2021.

30 The demon's name is Rahu. He swallows the sun and moon as retaliation for being denied an elixir. https://www.google.com/amp/s/www.indiatoday.in/amp/lifestyle/culture/story/total-solar-eclipse-indian-hindu-myths-superstitions-rahu-surya-grahan-religious-rituals-lifest-1030644-2017-08-21. Accessed April 22, 2021.

31 Shemal in Arabic. *History of the Arabian Mission.* p. 116.

32 *Independent.* March 1, 1899. p. 2.

33 Ibid.

34 Samuel M. Zwemer. *Raymund Lull: The First Missionary to the Moslems.* New York: Funk & Wagnalls Company, 1902. p. 145.

35 George E. Stone. "First Experiences, January 2, 1899." *The Arabian Mission: Quarterly Letters from the Field.* 28 (1898). p. 14-15.

36 Ibid.

37 *Independent.* March 1, 1899. p. 2.

38 *History of the Arabian Mission.* p. 116. George's December 25 letter and his "First Experience" article give a confusing timeline for the Thoms' arrival. The letter includes January 3, and he states the steamer arrived that day. The article is dated January 2 and probably completed on the 3.

39 Also spelled Seso.

40 The excerpt printed "C.B.C.F.M." which is a typographical error. It should be A.B.C.F.M—American Board of Commissioners of Foreign Missions.

41 He had a blacksmith's tools in mind.

42 *Independent.* March 22, 1899. p. 5.

43 Ibid.

44 Ibid.

45 Another spelling is "toweelah." Samuel Zwemer sent one of the coins to the American Bible Society. It was thought to be a thousand years old, but still used in some parts of Arabia. It was worth about a quarter of a cent for buying rice and dates. It consisted of "a small copper bar, with a small proportion of silver, about an inch in length, split at one end, and with a fissure slightly opened. Along one or both of its flattened sides run a few Cufic characters, nearly illegible in most specimens, but said to read, 'Mohammed of the Saood family.' The coin has neither date nor motto, but was undoubtedly struck by one of the Carmathian Princes about the year 920 A. D." "A Rare, Antique Coin." *Bible Society Record.* 24 (1899): 106-107. Accessed at books.google.com April 26, 2021.

46 Ras Ruman was a separate village in 1899. Manama's urban area today engulfs it. The name means "head of pomegranate." https://www.gdnonline.com/Details/361613/Restoring-Ras-Ruman. Accessed April 28, 2021.

47 *Independent.* March 22, 1899. p. 5.

Chapter 15: Take Up the Work

1. *Independent.* March 22, 1899. p. 5.
2. The family used the word "Sincere," which did not fit with the first two nouns.
3. *Independent.* March 22, 1899, p. 5. The YMCA week of prayer held November 13-19 may have been what George had in mind. The seven topics he referred to were Young men, the part they play in the Family, in the Church, in the Country; Life with Christ in the Spirit of Prayer; Life with Christ in His communion with God; Life with Christ in His separation from the world; Life with Christ in His brotherly love; Life with Christ in His love for the world; and Life with Christ in His consecration to God. *The New York Observer.* July 7, 1898. p. 15.
4. *Independent.* March 22, 1899. p. 5.
5. Copy of letter to President Stryker. Courtesy of Hamilton College Archives.
6. Ibid.
7. Rev. A. N. Petersen. "In Memory of Rev. George E. Stone." *Hamilton Literary Magazine.* November 1899. p. 104.
8. *Manual of the Board of Foreign Missions of the Reformed Church in America, For the Use of Missionaries Under Appointment and in Their Field of Labor.* New York: Press of Rogers and Sherwood Printing Co., 1895. p. 9.
9. "Field Notes—Arabian Mission: Muscat." *The Mission Field.* 11.6 (1898): 187.
10. *Independent.* April 12, 1899. p. 6. George quoted the orders in his February 17 letter to his parents.
11. *Arabia, The Cradle of Islam.* p. 372.
12. https://epod.usra.edu/blog/2019/01/bioluminescent-phytoplankton-in-the-persian-gulf-and-orion-overhead.html. Accessed May 3, 2021.
13. This letter became the most quoted one in literature following George's death. *Auburn Seminary Review.* 3.2 (1899): 70-71. https://babel.hathitrust.org/cgi/pt?id=hvd.ah3nr3&view=1up&seq=82. Accessed June 26, 2021. "Extract from a Letter of Rev. George E. Stone, February 17th, 1899, to the 'Auburn Seminary Review.'" *The Arabian Mission: Quarterly Letters from the Field.* 30 (1899): 6.

14 Letter to Rev. L. P. Davidson ('97 Auburn) probably written in the first week of June because George speaks of the four months in Muscat. *Auburn Seminary Review*. 3.5 (1899): 195-96.

PART IV: MUSCAT, OMAN
Chapter 16: An International Showdown

1. Judson I. Stone. *A Last Chapter of the Greatest Generation.* New York: Aviva Publishing, 2016. p. 93-94.
2. PAT 1.2 Public Domain World Maps. http://ian.macky.net/pat
3. *The Arabian Mission's Story.* p. 119.
4. Ibid. p. 120.
5. Ibid. p. 121.
6. Ibid. p. 122.
7. W. D. Peyton. *Old Oman.* London: Stacey International, 1983. p. 8.
8. https://om.usembassy.gov/gift-from-sultan. Accessed May 5, 2021.
9. https://www.state.gov/u-s-relations-with-oman. Accessed May 5, 2021. "The United States in World History." https://www.sqcc.org/wp-content/uploads/2020/07/VoyageofPeacock.pdf. Accessed May 5, 2021.
10. Hermann Frederick Eilts. *A Friendship Two Centuries Old: The United States and The Sultanate of Oman.* Sultan Qaboos Center and The Middle East Institute, Washington, DC, 1990. p. 8-15. https://www.mei.edu/sites/default/files/mei_library/pdf/23681.pdf. Accessed May 5, 2021.
11. Ibid. p. 15.
12. Publications, Newspaper cuttings, Photographs and correspondence about Persia and the Persian Gulf [400r] (813/878), British Library: India Office Records and Private Papers, Mss Eur F111/356, in Qatar Digital Library. https://qdl.qa/en/archive/81055/vdc_100109762422.0x000005. Accessed August 3, 2021.
13. *The Arabian Mission's Story.* p. 123.
14. "Oman Old Photos." https://omansilver.com/contents/en-us/d20_Oman_old_photos.html. Accessed December 5, 2022. "Bayt" means house.
15. Letter to Dr. Cobb, Foreign Mission Board Corresponding Secretary, RCA. Arabian Mission, 753, Box 1 and 2, folders 15, 18, 19.

16   The French received permission to use a coaling station in al-Makalla Cove in August 1900. Y. A. al-Ghailani. "Oman and the Franco-British Colonial Rivalry: The Bandar al-Jissah Cove 1898-1900. http://adabjournal.uofk.edu/current%20issue/issues%20english/Dr.%20y.a.%20al-ghailani.pdf. Accessed May 5, 2021.

Chapter 17: House Repairs and Slave School

1   Archibald MacKirdy was Scottish. George wrote his last name as MacKirdy in his March 11 letter. https://politicalgraveyard.com/bio/mackenzie-macksey.html/#Mackirdy. Accessed May 15, 2021. His name is spelled McCurdy in other literature. He served as the agent for the mail steamers, as well as for American importing and exporting. *The Golden Milestone.* p. 41, 99.

2   Following Peter's death, two of the oldest boys wrote to Rev. Cantine expressing their sadness. They thought of Peter when they sang the songs he had taught them. *History of the Arabian Mission.* p. 96.

3   George gave their names as Leyid Ali and Ali Gemaal.

4   These titles were used for Europeans, especially Britons, in the Middle East and India. Mem referred to a woman or wife. "Sahib." *Merriam-Webster.com Dictionary.* Merriam-Webster. https://www.merriam-webster.com/dictionary/sahib. Accessed May 6, 2021.

5   George's quarterly letter written at the end of March. "Muscat." *The Arabian Mission: Quarterly Letters from the Field.* No. 29. p. 5-6.

6   *History of the Arabian Mission.* p. 96-97. Used by permission. Reformed Church in America, Global Mission Department.

7   *History of the Arabian Mission.* p. 90-91.

8   *Independent.* April 12, 1899. p. 6.

9   Ibid.

10 See *History of the Arabian Mission*, p. 48-50, for a brief summary of Bishop French's ministry in India and travels in the Persian Gulf region, where he met Rev. James Cantine and Rev. Samuel Zwemer, before dying on April 14, 1891.

11 He adapted Hebrews 11:4 to write of Peter Zwemer and Bishop French.

12 See 2 Peter 1:19.

13 Galatians 6:9.

14. Psalm 125:2.
15. *Mexico: Mother of Towns.* p. 353; *Independent.* January 11, 1899. p. 8.
16. *Independent.* May 17, 1899. p. 4.
17. He was appointed Vice Consul in the early 1880s. https://books.google.com/books?id=Q88-AAAAYAAJ&pg=PA173&lpg=PA173&dq=alexander+mackirdy,+muscat&source=bl&ots=5rTYfTaA_h&sig=ACfU3UruR9vzbFcOCvH4BVc10TXenso8g&hl=e&sa=X&ved=2ahUKEwiQvdvxqMzwAhXbbc)KHQXzDlgQ6AEwBxoECA4QAg#v=onepage&q=alexander%20mackirdy%2C%20muscat&f=false. Accessed May 18, 2021.
18. Archibald MacKirdy saw a picture of Ms. Olive Malvery in the April 15, 1903, edition of the London weekly *Tatler.* He met her when she was a child in India, where she was born. He wrote to her in England, and they married June 2, 1905, at St. Margaret's, Westminster. Three children were born to them before he died in 1909. https://www.olivemalvery.com/timeline. Accessed May 18, 2021.
19. The testimony of a resident. *Arabia: The Cradle of Islam.* p. 80.
20. George's estimated rainfall is more than twice the amount listed at https://www.climatestotravel.com/climate/oman#muscat. Accessed July 27, 2021.
21. *Independent.* January 11, 1899. p. 8.
22. The mixture included quinine, calomel, rhubarb, jalop, and opium. "Livingstone Rousers, I presume…" https://www.antiquestradegazette.com/news/2002/livingstone-rousers-i-presume/. Accessed May 18, 2021.
23. "Muscat." *The Arabian Mission: Quarterly Letters from the Field.* 29 (1899): 5-6.
24. Ibid.
25. It is also spelled Hilawi and Halwa, a popular sweet made from dates.
26. *Arabia: Cradle of Islam.* p. 81.
27. For a contemporary hike, see "Go on a Coastal Trek on Sidab, Oman." *Oman Magazine.* https://omanmagazine.com/explore/go-on-a-coastal-trek-in-sidab-oman/. Accessed May 20, 2021.
28. May have been the HMS *Sphinx.*
29. *Arabia: Cradle of Islam.* p. 82.

Chapter 18: Eyes on Calendar and Thermometer

1. *History of the Arabian Mission.* p. 79, 92.
2. Unidentified. Wali can mean authority, governor, custodian, protector; or a person responsible for a Muslim bride before marriage. https://www.definitions.net/definition/WALI. Accessed September 7, 2022.
3. Surah 5:68; Surah 10:94.
4. *Independent.* June 28, 1899. p. 4.
5. Ergun Mehmet Caner and Emir Fethi Caner. *Unveiling Islam: An Insider's Look at Muslim Life and Beliefs.* Grand Rapids, Michigan: Kregel Publications, 2002. p. 154-56.
6. Letters to Dr. Cobb, April 21 and May 6, 1899. RCA Archives, Arabian Mission, 753, Box 1-2, Folders 15, 18, 19.
7. George's letter to Dr. Cobb, May 6, 1899. RCA Archives, Arabian Mission, 753, Box 1-2, Folders 15, 18, 19.
8. Rev. Leonard Palmeter Davidson (1866-1901). Studied at Union Theological Seminary 1897-98; served in Indiana (1898-99); married in 1898; his wife died in 1899; served in Manila, Philippines 1900-01. Died on June 8, 1901. *General biographical catalogue of Auburn Theological Seminary 1818-1918.* Auburn, NY: Auburn Seminary Press, 1918. p. 245. "Leonard Palmeter Davidson – Facts." https://www.ancestry.com/family-tree/person/tree/116644762/person/202238921970/facts. Accessed July 15, 2021.
9. George wrote in April that he had two or three fevers, "small affairs." *Arabia: The Cradle of Islam.* p. 372.
10. *Auburn Seminary Review.* 3.5 (1899): 195-96.

PART V: DEATH AND BURIAL
Chapter 19: A Most Grievous Blow

1. The Rev. William H. Mason, George's seminary classmate, wrote of the cablegram, "creeping stealthily along under the ocean, striking at last like the crack of doom on our shores, came the two electric words, 'Stone dead.' What a fatal message!" *Independent.* August 9, 1899. p. 8.
2. *Independent.* July 5, 1899.
3. It was later than he originally planned. See above in the month of

4 *Golden Milestone.* p. 98.
5 "Muscat." *The Arabian Mission Quarterly Letters from the Field.* 31 (1899): p. 3.
6 *Golden Milestone.* p. 98.
7 PAT 1.2 Public Domain World Maps http://ian.macky.net/pat.
8 Rev. Cantine included this note with his letter to George's parents. *Independent.* August 9, 1899. p. 1. He wrote in *Golden Milestone* (p. 98) that George wrote "letters" from Birka in which he expressed appreciation for the change in scenery and that his health was fair. Cantine also stated that George was gone for two or three weeks, but this was not the case. They traveled to Birka on June 22, four days before his death.
9 *Golden Milestone.* p. 98.
10 1865-1929. Commanded the *Pigeon* from March 31, 1897—December 31, 1899. http://www.dreadnoughtproject.org/tfs/index/H.M.S._Pigeon_(1888). Accessed August 11, 2021.
11 *Independent.* August 9, 1899. p. 1.
12 "A potentially fatal response to excess heat outside the body; heatstroke. A nonspecific term for any cyclical fever occurring in malaria; ardent fever." https://medical-dictionary.thefreedictionary.com/heat+apoplexy. Accessed May 22, 2021.
13 *Independent.* August 9, 1899. p. 1.
14 Ibid.

Chapter 20: Memorial Service and Tributes

1 Letter to Dr. Cobb, June 30, 1899. *Arabian Mission papers, 1890-1946,* RCA Archives. Box 754.
2 *Independent.* July 5, 1899. p. 8.
3 N. W. Wolcott, pastor of the Baptist church; Rev. Theodore L. Allen, rector of Grace Episcopal Church; and Rev. J. H. Myers, Methodist Church minister.
4 https://www.newhopeparish.org/history. Accessed May 25, 2021.
5 *Independent.* July 5, 1899, p. 1.

6 Ephesians 3:8.
7 *Independent.* July 5, 1899. p. 1.
8 Ibid.
9 Hebrews 11:4.
10 "May he rest in peace." RIP. "Requiescat in pace." *Merriam-Webster.com Dictionary,* Merriam Webster, https://merriam-webster.com/dictionary/requiescat%20in%20pace. Accessed May 25, 2021.
11 *Independent,* July 5, 1899, p. 1.
12 *Pulaski Democrat.* July 12, 1899, p.3. The cousin was Mrs. Sarah Jennie Pierce Beeman (1856-1944). She was the daughter of Sarah Ames Stone Pierce (1823-1884), George's aunt, who was thirteen years older than George's father. "North America, Family Histories, 1500-2000." https://www.ancestry.com/imageviewer/collections/61157/images/46155_b290502-00441?usePUB=true&usePUBJs=true&pId=4045261. Accessed July 16, 2021.
13 Rev. Dorr served the Methodist Episcopal Church in Mexico in 1891-93. He knew George and his family. "Methodist Episcopal Church, Mexico, NY http://sites.rootsweb.com/~nyoswego/towns/mexico/methepiscopal.html. Accessed June 8, 2021.
14 *Independent.* July 12, 1899, p. 4. Rev. Samuel Zwemer also quoted this verse in his memorial tribute to George in *Arabia: The Cradle of Islam,* p. 373.
15 "Rev. George E. Stone." *The Evangelist.* 70.29 (1899): 18-19.

Chapter 21: More Tributes

1 A scene in the 2019 movie *The Last Full Measure.* The movie was Peter Fonda and Christopher Plummer's last movie. The movie includes Ed Harris and Samuel L. Jackson.
2 *Independent.* August 9, 1899. p. 1. The Stones adapted Job's statement with the plural pronouns.
3 Ibid. August 9, 1899. p. 1.
4 His grave was not lonely. The cemetery contained many graves.
5 *Independent.* August 9, 1899. p. 1.
6 Alfred Lord Tennyson's friend and fellow poet. https://www.britannica.com/biography/Arthur-henry-hallam. Accessed June 5, 2021.

7   *Independent.* August 9, 1899. p. 1.

8   Ibid.

9   See Chapter 6, above.

10 *Independent.* August 9, 1899. p. 5.

11 "O Love, that wilt not let me go," by Rev. George Matheson, DD (1842-1906), a blind pastor. His sister, who had been his helper, was leaving him to get married. He was deeply distressed by this matter. He reported that the words came to him quickly. Charles Seymour Robinson, DD. *Annotations upon Popular Hymns.* Cincinnati, OH: Cranston & Curts, 1893. p. 518. Brian Cochran. "Historical Background for the Hymn: 'O Love That Will Not Let Me Go.' https://www.google.com/amp/s/wrathtoriches.wordpress.com/2013/04/24/o-love-that-will-not-let-me-go/amp/. Accessed June 1, 2021.

12 *Independent.* August 9, 1899. p. 5.

13 Ibid. August 9, 1899. p. 5. The dispatch was dated June 27. The notice misspelled Mr. Archibald MacKirdy's last name as MacKirby.

14 "In Memory to Rev. George E. Stone." *Hamilton Literary Magazine.* November 1899. p. 101-104.

15 Ibid. Rev. Petersen became a Protestant chaplain at Sing Sing Prison for twenty-five years. He followed his own advice to the students, dying in 1940.

16 *The Arabian Mission: Quarterly Letters from the Field.* 33 (1900): 10. Rev. F. J. Barny authored the Resolution. Later, he completed *The History of the Arabian Mission.* George's middle name was spelled as Edwin, instead of Erwin. The town where George died is also spelled Bisket, instead of Birka.

17 Luke 5:28, King James Version.

18 *The Arabian Mission: Quarterly Letters from the Field.* 36 (1900): 4. The verse is taken from Luke 5:28 (KJV).

19 *Golden Milestone.* p. 98-99.

20 Ibid.

21 *History of the Arabian Mission. p. 105.*

22 *Golden Milestone.* p. 102-103.

23 *The Arabian Mission: Quarterly Letters from the Field.* January – March

1900, No. 33. p. 8.

24 "Home and Family Life," Chapter XVII, Part II, *Apostle to Islam,* digital edition, 2016.

25 *Golden Milestone.* p. 104-105.

26 *History of the Arabian Mission.* p. 133.

Chapter 22: The Family Carries On

1 New York, U.S., Wills and Probate Records, 1659-1999. www.ancestry.com. Accessed June 26, 2021.

2 He served in the Hoboken, New Jersey area when the American soldiers shipped out to Europe in 1917-18. He saw his nephew Elmore Stone, a member of the New York 51st Pioneer Infantry Regiment, before boarding a ship for France in September 1918.

3 *Independent.* August 16, 1899. p. 4.

4 Ibid. September 27, 1899. p. 3. There is no mention in the paper that George and Sophie attended.

5 Ibid. October 18, 1899. p. 4.

6 Ibid. November 9, 1899. p. 2.

7 Ibid. August 22, 1900. p. 1.

8 Ibid. September 19, 1900. p. 3.

9 Ibid. August 28, 1901. p. 3. Walter Stone worked at the Mexico *Independent* for four years before leaving Mexico in 1871. In 1873, he moved to Camden, started a weekly newspaper, and then purchased the *Journal* and merged the two papers. http://www.onlinebiographies.info/ny/onei/stone-wc.htm. Accessed June 8, 2021.

10 Rev. Cantine's daily scheduler mentions arriving in Mexico, speaking, and departing. Zwemer's diary is missing his visit, as well as other dates that coincide with George's connection to him. Courtesy of Rev. Adam Simnowitz, Dearborn, Michigan, who is a writer for the *Journal of Biblical Missiology.* www.biblicalmissiology.org.

11 Caroline L. Smith (1852). It was recast in 1885, then altered and published in 1900. https://library.timelesstruths.org/music/tarry_with_me/. Accessed June 10, 2021.

12 *Independent.* July 22, 1903. p. 1.

13 Ibid. July 26, 1905. p. 2; August 2, 1905. p. 8.

14 Ibid. p. 2.

15 *History of the Arabian Mission.* p. 128; *The Arabian Mission's Story.* p. 192. By 1905, in addition to his daughters, Zwemer lost four fellow missionaries—his brother Peter, George Stone, Henry Wiersum, and Dr. Marion Thoms. Scudder discusses the impact these losses may have had on Samuel and Amy. *The Arabian Mission's Story,* p. 189-191, n. 168.

16 1900 Federal Census. He is listed as an insurance agent. www.ancestry.com.

17 "Memorial at Athenia Church." *The Christian Intelligencer and Mission Field.* 99.23 (1928): p. 359.

PART VI: REV. GEORGE E. STONE'S LEGACY
Chapter 23: His Legacy in Literature

1 New York, NY: Fleming H. Revell Company, 1900. p. 371-73. The first part of the chapter is devoted to Rev. Peter J. Zwemer who died in October 1898. George is also mentioned on p. 351, 366.

2 The date given for his birth, September 2, 1870, is incorrect. He was born September 1, 1873. p. 371.

3 Ibid. p. 372.

4 Ibid. p. 373.

5 "Rev. George E. Stone." *Acts and Proceedings of the Reformed Church in America.* Vol. XIX, New York: Board of Publication of the Reformed Church in America, 1901. p. 903-904. The cove shoreline is composed of small smooth rocks today. Trash washes up on the shore. I brought home a fishing lure, a rock, piece of coral, and a shell.

6 Rev. Wiersum arrived on the field in December 1899 and began his language training. He died of a virulent attack of smallpox on August 3, 1901. "Busrah: Mr. Wiersum—His Life and Death." *The Arabian Mission: Quarterly Letters from the Field.* 39 (1901): 3-5.

7 Ibid. p. 5.

8 Ibid. "The Arabian Mission: A Statement." p. 17.

9 Samuel M. Zwemer. *Islam: A Challenge of Faith.* New York: Student Volunteer Movement for Foreign Missions. 2nd ed. 1909. p. 200.

10 Rev. Zwemer received an invitation from the National Christian Council of India, and on behalf of the American Christian Literature

Society for Moslems, to visit India. Before arriving in India, they visited Jerusalem, Beirut, Baghdad, Busrah, Kuwait, Bushire, Bahrain, and Muscat. Samuel Zwemer. *Report of a Visit to Mesopotamia the Persian Gulf and India*. New York, NY: The American Christian Literature Society for Moslems, 1924. p. 3, 5.

11 *Apostle to Islam.* p. 153-54.

12 Galatians 6:9.

13 *Outlines of Missionary History.* New York, NY: G. H. Doran, 1912.

14 *History of the Arabian Mission.* p. 91, 98-102, 243. George's middle name is incorrectly listed as "Edwin" instead of Erwin on p. 243.

15 *The Celebration of the Centennial Anniversary of the Founding of the Mexico Academy August 15-19, 1926.* Mexico, NY: Alumni Association, 1927. p. 39. It is worth noting that Laura Fish taught at the school. She married Dr. Garrett P. Judd, and they served as missionaries to the Sandwich Islands, which we know as Hawai'i, from 1828 until their deaths in 1872 (Laura) and 1873 (Garrett). See *Mexico Mother of Towns* for a brief reference to this couple on p. 429.

16 *Independent.* August 20, 1926. p. 7.

17 *Golden Milestone.* p. 42.

18 "Half-Century Annalist Letters—1895 Class Annalist's Letter." Hamilton College. https://my.hamilton.edu/about/history/half-century-annalists-letters/1895. Accessed July 29, 2021.

19 *Mexico-Mother of Towns.* p. 275.

20 The author learned much by reading and researching details in George's letters. Arthur Berry's letters are just as fascinating.

21 *Arab World Pioneers* series. Published by Pioneer Library. First digital edition, 2016. p. 154.

22 Acknowledgements. p. iii. Lewis R. Scudder. *The Arabian Mission's Story.* p. 407. Scudder mentions Tameemi in the lengthy note 168 on p. 191 and note 6 on p. 417. He spells his name Abd-ul-Mâlik at-TamÎmÎ.

23 Tamm, Abdal-Malik Khalat. *The Arabian Mission: A Case Study of Christian Missionary Work in the Arabian Gulf Region.* Durham thesis, Durham University, 1978. Available at Durham E-Theses Online: http://etheses.dur.ac.uk/3601/

24 Ibid. p. 1.

25 Ibid. p. 211-12.

26 This letter became the most quoted one in literature following George's death. *Auburn Seminary Review*. 3.2 (1899): 70-71. https://babel.hathitrust.org/cgi/pt?id=hvd.ah3nr3&view=1up&seq=82. Accessed June 26, 2021. "Extract from a Letter of Rev. George E. Stone, February 17th, 1899, to the 'Auburn Seminary Review.'" *The Arabian Mission: Quarterly Letters from the Field*. 30 (1899): 6.

27 Rev. James Cantine. "Muscat," *Neglected Arabia: Quarterly Letters and News of the Arabian Mission*. 52 (1904): 7.

28 Al-Tamini. p. 45-46. In a note at the bottom of p. 45, he says, "Mr. Stone was one of the pioneers of the Arabian Mission. He worked in Muscat for a short period in 1899, then he gave up because of illness, and died the next year." He does not cite a source for the claim that George gave up. There is no evidence for this claim. Cantine never stated that he gave up. Also, George died in 1899, not the next year.

29 Ibid. p. 22.

30 Matthew, Mark, Luke, John, Acts, Romans, 1 & 2 Corinthians, Galatians, Ephesian, Philippians, Colossians, 1 Thessalonians, 1 Timothy ("who gave himself as a ransom," 2:6), 2 Timothy, Titus ("gave himself for us," 2:14), Hebrews, 1 Peter, 1 John, Revelation.

31 Sura XIX: 33; Sura IV: 156: "They did not slay him (Jesus) neither crucified him, only a likeness of that was shown to them." The verse (aye) in the second Sura is numbered 157 in M. H. Shahir's edition of *The Qur'an*. 12th edition. Elmhurst, NY: Tahrike Tarsile Qur'an, 2001.

32 Al-Tamīnī. p. 23.

33 Lewis R. Scudder. *The Arabian Mission's Story: In Search of Abraham's Other Son*. Grand Rapids, MI.: Wm. B. Eerdmans, 1998.

34 *The Arabian Mission's Story*. p. 417-19.

35 Ibid. p. 38. n. 60. He incorrectly states that George arrived in Muscat in February 1898 (p. 171), and that he died June 28 (p. 172). He correctly lists his date of death as June 26 on p. 528. On p. 528, George's middle initial should be E.

36 Ibid. p. 192.

37 "A Historical Survey of US-Omani Relations from 1790 to the Present." *Oman and Overseas: Studies on Ibadism and Oman*. Vol. 2. Eds. Abdulrahman Al-Salimi and Michaela Hoffman-Ruf. New York: Georg Olms Verlag, 2013. p. 437-48.

38 Rev. Cantine served about nine years, beginning in 1898, with assignments to other stations and a furlough in the USA. See Scudder p. 528-530.

39 Personal email from Rev. Leonard, dated August 13, 2021.

40 Personal email dated August 12, 2021.

41 *A Last Chapter of the Greatest Generation: The Life and Family of Colonel Frederic A. Stone, M.D.* Lake Placid, NY: Aviva Publishing, 2016. p. 24-26. His middle name is mistakenly given as Edwin instead of Erwin. I failed to include Dr. John Lansing as a founder of the Mission. These mistakes show I did not know George or the Mission thoroughly enough to write more than I did.

42 Sarah Rose. *D-Day Girls*. New York, NY: Broadway Books, 2020. p. 30.

43 June 30, 1899. RCA Archives, 753, Box 1-2, Folders 15, 18, 19.

44 Scudder. *The Arabian Mission's Story*. p. 171, n. 119; p. 324, n. 3.

45 Cambridge Scholars Publishing. p. 11. https://www.cambridgescholars.com/resources/pdfs/978-1-5275-1131-6-sample.pdf. Accessed June 24, 2021.

46 *Left to Tell*. New York, NY: Hay House, 2006. p. 209-10.

Chapter 24: Willing for It to Be So

1 Isaiah 40: 6-8.

2 Vivienne Stacey. *Thomas Valpy French, First Bishop of Lahore*. p. 115. http://www.stfrancismagazine.info/ja/Biography%20of%20Thomas%20Valpy%20French.pdf. Accessed February 8, 2023.

3 Ibid. p. 117-18. *History of the Arabian Mission*, p. 48-50. *The Arabian Mission's Story*, p. 149-51.

4 Charles Thomas Wilson. *Alexander Mackay: Missionary Hero of Uganda*. London, Gr. Brit.: The Sunday School Union. Kessinger Legacy Reprints. p. 21.

5 Ibid. p. 142.

6 Kevin Belmonte. *Beacon-Light: The Life of William Borden (1887-1913)*. Great Brit.: Geanies House, Fearn, Ross-shire, Gr. Brit.: Christian Focus Publications, Ltd, 2021, p. 239ff.

7 "Memorial Service for John W. O'Brien." *Hamilton Literary Magazine*. 29.8 (1896): 297.

8 Quoted in *Out of the Blue by* Greg Murtha. p. 185.

9   "For the Fallen" (1914); quoted in William Barclay, *John.*, Vol 2. p. 172.
10 George is listed as the third pastor of the Protestant Church in Oman. Https://www.churchinoman.com/our-history.
11 "25 Carter G. Woodson Quotes About Knowing Black History." https://everydaypower.com/carter-g-woodson-quotes. Accessed February 16, 2023.
12 *The Arabian Mission's Story.* p. 557.
13 *Raymund Lull.* p. 1-2.
14 *The History of the Arabian Mission.* p. 101.

About the Author

The Rev. Dr. Judson I. Stone is the author of the biography of his father, *A Last Chapter of the Greatest Generation: The Life and Family of Colonel Frederic A. Stone, M.D. Aviator, Doctor, Missionary, and Friend to Humanity* (2016). His next project is to complete a biography of a great-uncle including the transcription of his World War I diary.

Judson volunteers at the Walton Correctional Institution in DeFuniak Springs, Florida, and at his church in Santa Rosa Beach. He retired as a corporate chaplain in Arlington, Texas. While there, he volunteered with the Fellowship of Christian Athletes as team chaplain in high school football and D-1 college basketball. He also taught at several Disciple Training Schools for Youth with a Mission in Hyderabad, India. Judson served as a pastor for twenty-six years in Maine. In 1992, he rode a bicycle from Dexter, Maine, to Anacortes, Washington, to raise funds for missions.

Judson is married to Jan, a retired nurse. They are the parents of three grown sons and grandparents to five grandchildren. He is a member of the Destin Word Weavers International Writers chapter.

Links to Judson's books can be found at https://JudsonIStone.com.

More Books by Rev. Judson I. Stone

If you enjoyed and were inspired by *A Modest But Crucial Hero*, you might also enjoy Rev. Stone's previous book:

A Last Chapter of the Greatest Generation:
The Life and Family of Colonel Frederic A. Stone, M.D.
Aviator, Doctor, Missionary, and Friend to Humanity

Take a seat on the flight to almost everywhere as Colonel Frederic A. Stone, M.D. grows into manhood fretting about what career path to take and thinking that a military track will limit his life experiences. He chooses the Army anyway in February 1941 and starts on the adventure of his life—one that will surprise even him and far exceed anything he could imagine. Visit places in the U.S. and around the world that you might never have known existed or even thought about visiting. Join this member of the greatest generation as he finds that dreams can be fulfilled in the most unexpected ways through a career, marriage and fatherhood, and ambitions.

The greatest generation is shrinking rapidly and Frederic A. Stone was a last chapter of it. He left a legacy in aviation, medicine, missions, and friendship to humanity. Let his story inspire you to trust in God with your dreams and ambitions. You, too, will be surprised on this flight to everywhere.

A Last Chapter of the Greatest Generation and all of Rev. Stone's books are available at:

https://JudsonIStone.com

www.ingramcontent.com/pod-product-compliance
Lightning Source LLC
Chambersburg PA
CBHW042320090526
44585CB00024BA/2656